ACRES OF GLASS

The Story of the Dale Estate
and How Brampton Became
"The Flower Town of Canada"

DALE O'HARA

eastendbooks
2007

Production and Design by Jeanne MacDonald and Randall White
Cover Concept by Diane Allengame
Edited by Donna Davies
Author's photograph courtesy of Finn O'Hara Photography

Printed in Canada

The author gratefully acknowledges the financial support of the City of Brampton and the Brampton Arts Council with a grant, which enabled the publication of this book.

Library and Archives Canada Cataloguing in Publication

O'Hara, Dale, 1942
    Acres of glass : the story of the Dale Estate and how Brampton became "The flower town of Canada" / Dale O'Hara

Includes bibliographical references and index.
ISBN 978-1-896973-39-5

    1. Dale Estate Nurseries (Brampton, Ont.) -- History
2. Nurseries (Horticulture) -- Ontario-- Brampton--History.
3. Dale family. I. Title

SB118. 75. C3043 2007   381' .415909713535   C2007-902565-X

eastendbooks
45 Fernwood Park Ave, Toronto, ON M4E3E9
Tel: (416) 691 6816 Fax: (416) 691 2414

In memory of my mother and father,
Elizabeth Dale Brydon and Douglas Morrison Dickson,
whose deep love of family
continues to be a constant source of inspiration.

"My name is Ozymandias, king of kings:
Look on my works, ye Mighty, and despair!"
Nothing beside remains. Round the decay
Of that colossal wreck, boundless and bare
The lone and level sands stretch far away.

Excerpt from "Ozymandias"
by Percy Bysshe Shelley
1792 – 1822

Table of Contents

The Corporation of the City of Brampton

Susan Fennell
Mayor

April 2007

On behalf of the City of Brampton and my colleagues on Council, I am pleased to offer my congratulations to Dale O'Hara, the author of "Acres of Glass" for her outstanding work in completing this important history of the Dale Estate. I would also like to express my thanks to the Brampton Arts Council for managing this book project, and the staff of the Peel Heritage Complex for their important contribution.

The cultivating of hothouse flowers was our city's largest industry throughout most of the 20th century, making Brampton both the flower production capital of the British Empire, and the Flower Town of Canada. With the demise of the domestic flower industry in Canada in the 1970's, this vital part of our city's history was all but lost, and I am so grateful to the author for reconnecting us with this incredible legacy!

Today, we have reclaimed our flower city heritage with a major focus on beautifying Brampton with floral displays across our city. In 2006, Brampton won the national Communities in Bloom Competition and is Canada's Flower Town once more. This important book will help us to celebrate our history and bridge our rich past to our promising future.

Warmest regards,

Susan D. Fennell

Susan Fennell
Mayor

Acknowledgements

In 2002 I decided to write a book about my family and the Dale Estate. I am two generations removed from some of the old time employees and I knew that time was running out to record their oral history. Little did I know the enthusiasm that would be generated as I undertook this project. Through many interviews with past employees, numerous phone calls from old Bramptonians, and contacts with long-lost cousins, stories have been unearthed and oral histories collaborated.

For everyone who accompanied me on the journey backwards in time, I thank you for sharing your gentle memories. Individual names are too numerous to mention but know that each of you contributed to this book with your wonderful gems of information helping me to flesh out the story of the Dale Estate.

In particular I wish to acknowledge the assistance I received from the staff and volunteers at the Peel Heritage Complex during my research. A treasure trove of information and people with unique skills are housed in that marvellous complex, without which this book could not have been written.

I especially want to thank Diane Allengame, Registrar of the Region of Peel Archives, who encouraged me to pursue the project. Diane has generously volunteered her time and expertise by scanning all of the images for the book using the Archive's state-of-the-art equipment. She has also proofread the manuscript for historical accuracy, had general input into the overall design and has given me her unwavering support and friendship every step of the way.

It was Diane who suggested that I contact Donna Davies to be my editor, a fortuitous introduction. Donna's encouragement and enthusiasm for the book bolstered my courage in thinking that I could write and renewed my faith that what I had written was worth reading. With her keen eye for design, grammar and clarity, we have crafted a wonderful story. She truly is an editor extraordinaire.

Donna in turn introduced me to my publisher Jeanne MacDonald of *eastendbooks* who worked hand in hand with Diane, Donna and me bringing the story to life through pictures and design. What a team we made, for this book has truly been a collaborative effort.

Part of this team effort has been the financial support of the City of Brampton and the Brampton Arts Council. Michael Halls embraced the project, Mayor Susan Fennell and City Council wholeheartedly backed it, Dennis Cutajar expedited the approval process and Marnie Richards worked on the minute details of the grant to produce the book. I thank them all.

And lastly, I'd like to acknowledge the support of my family, in particular my husband Errill. Without their belief and pride in what I do, I could not have written *Acres of Glass*.

As in all histories, although this book is based on fact and has been researched to the best of my ability, some assumptions have been made and inevitably errors may have occurred, for which I take sole responsibility. I hope you enjoy my story of the Dales and the early days of "The Flower Town of Canada" and that it evokes within you wonderful memories of a bygone era.

Introduction

Throughout most of the last century, Brampton enjoyed an international reputation as "The Flower Town of Canada." Acre upon acre of glass greenhouses filled almost every nook and cranny of the town and, at one point, there were over 48 nurseries whose businesses were devoted to the growing of hothouse flowers. The largest of these was the Dale Estate located at the northern limits of the town occupying both sides of the main street, with greenhouses stretching east to the Etobicoke Creek and west to the CPR rail line. Royalty, heads of government, business leaders and movie stars, among others, all made their way to tour the greenhouses of the Dale Estate, especially to see the famous Dale Autographed Roses and the over 500,000 orchid plants. At the height of its productivity, the Dale Estate had 140 greenhouses with over 1.5 million square feet of glass, and had bragging rights as the largest cut flower business on the continent and the third largest in the world. They were famous for their huge production of over 20 million blooms, the quality and prestige of their roses, and for introducing innumerable new species of roses and orchids for the mass market.

Most of the men and women who worked at the Dale Estate have passed on, but many of those remaining still recall the acres of greenhouses, the tunnels, the steam pipes, the Dale whistle, the Dale chimney and the Dale family. The mothers, fathers, aunts, uncles, cousins and neighbours who worked there have fond memories of a company

In 1988 a former employee wrote to Doug Dickson, Vice-President of the Dale Estate.
Courtesy Dale O'Hara Collection.

that treated them with respect and produced some of the finest flowers in the world, and they remember a small town called Brampton.

The Story Behind a Company and a Town

Behind every great enterprise such as the Dale Estate there is a story. This story is about Harry Dale, an Englishman from humble beginnings, who had a deep-seated love of roses, and who was filled with the entrepreneurial spirit that symbolized Canada in the early years of immigration. It is a story that parallels the growth of Brampton from a small village to an internationally known town, with the two entities enjoying a close symbiotic relationship. It is a story about the Dales, a family that experienced personal tragedies as well as triumphs. It is about the floral empire they built, which was known for over a century throughout North America and Europe for its highly-prized, award winning roses, and then, within a span of ten years, it disappeared. Their 35 acres of greenhouses were abandoned, their international reputation was forgotten and not a trace of their former company remained. It is hard to believe that a business of such magnitude and reputation could be so rapidly and completely dismantled.

Today we are witness to the intrinsic floral legacy left by the Dale Estate, which is manifested in the ongoing revitalization of the city's heritage

This, then, is the story of the Dale Estate and its influence on the development of Brampton as "The Flower Town of Canada."

Chapter 1

Emigration from England
1850 — 1863

Noteworthy Events of the Time

1851 County of Peel formed

1853 Brampton incorporated as a village

1854 Crimean War begins

1858 Cariboo Gold Rush

1859 Proposed merger of Upper and Lower Canada

1861 American Civil War begins

L ife for young Harry Dale's father, Edward, in 1850s England was becoming increasingly difficult. The industrial revolution, which was sweeping the realm, was bringing new mechanized machinery to the farms, replacing many workers as well as changing the economy of the countryside. Periods of drought followed by excessive rainfall were taking their toll on the fields and farms, the source of the Dale family's income. Epidemics of typhoid, cholera, influenza and tuberculosis were rampant not only in the overcrowded cities but in the towns as well, an ever-present worry to a man with young children. In addition, wages for farmers and gardeners, such as the Dales, were extremely low and, unless there were sons that could be sent out to work, making ends meet was a challenge for a young family.

Tradesmen of West Street

Edward Dale and his father William made their living as market gardeners in Dorking, located in Surrey near the south coast of England. Dorking was an ancient market town with the surrounding rich fields growing many of the vegetables to supply the large London market.

The family lived on West Street, one of the oldest streets in Dorking, where mostly tradesmen were housed in tenements converted from the large buildings of the Tudor period. At number 87 lived the wheelwright Tindle, his wife and their unmarried daughter; across the road at number 88 lived the widower Owen Croucher and his five children, one of whom worked as a porter; and at number 90 lived William Tenor, a landholder, and his unmarried daughter Maria. At 91 West Street was the Rose and Crown Public House, offering room and board as well as food and ale, ably run by Thomas Guinfiste and his wife Jane. Finally came the Dale clan at number 89, with Edward, his wife Sarah, and their three children, Henry aged ten, Sarah aged two and Ann aged one, as well as his father, William Dale.[1] West Street, with its cramped living quarters, formed one side of the market area, and served as the focal point of entertainment and lifestyle for the surrounding area. Henry, whom everyone called Harry, attended the local school and in all probability helped Edward in the market gardens in the surrounding countryside. Whether they owned the gardens or not is unknown, but what is known is that Edward became extremely knowledgeable about growing and marketing vegetables.

By early 1860, Edward could see that the future as a market gardener for him and his young family was bleak, because with the advent of trains to Dorking the area became easily accessible and a highly desirable place for Londoners to live. As a result the surrounding farmlands were in high demand for building stately homes for those wishing to escape the large city for the quieter countryside. Although this growth ensured the survival of the town with its charm and beauty, which remains to the present day, it began to force out the market gardening operations that for generations had sustained the Dale family.

Fortunes to be Made in Canada

Stories of cheap land and fortunes to be made were coming from Canada. Faced with the prospect of continuing low wages for heavy work as a gardener,[2] possible death of family members from disease and the changing face of market gardening practices, Edward decided to pack up his family and move, with hopes of creating a better life for himself and his children. Edward is a prime example of the pioneering spirit that shaped Canada and much of North America in the 19th century.

Edward Dale booked passage for his family and set sail for America on May 20, 1863, arriving in New York on June 20, after a long, four-week crossing. The hardships of travelling with four young children, one a mere baby, can only be imagined. After recovering their land legs, the family boarded a train to Toronto with plans to continue on to the village known as Brampton. Edward's decision to settle there as a final destination can only be speculated upon, as there is no record of other relatives living in the area. Perhaps it was through government advertising, or through a letter from a friend, or simply because Edward knew that Brampton held all of the ingredients to establish a business, as in 1863 the village was poised on the cusp of great prosperity.

Growth of Brampton

Begun at a crossroads in the early 1820s, Brampton was in the heart of what had become one of the richest agricultural areas in Upper Canada. In 1850 the population had grown to 550 from approximately 100 people twelve years previously. Three years later in 1853 Brampton was incorporated as a village with the early pioneer families of Elliot, Howland, Holmes, Lynch and Lawson, who had settled there, establishing Brampton as a destination of choice. Several factors came into play that enabled the village to grow, the main one of which was an improvement in transportation. By 1853

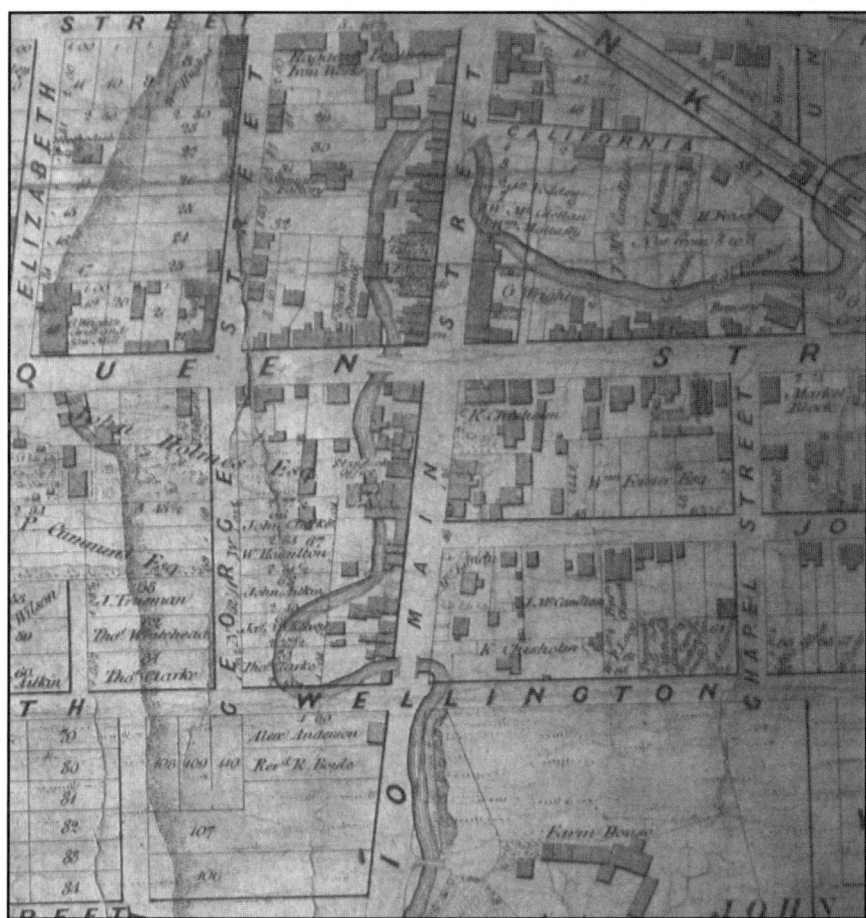

An early map of Brampton shows the concentration of businesses around the intersection of Main and Queen streets, 1857.
Courtesy Brampton Historical Society/Region of Peel Archives ("RPA")

As Brampton grew it attracted many merchants, such as Golding, Shenich and Stork, whose stores lined the main streets of the village, 1859. Courtesy Tremaine Map/RPA

the Hurontario Plank Road Company had planked Brampton's main street all the way from Port Credit to what is now Mayfield Road, a huge improvement over dirt trails. This plank road proved to be neither reliable in wet weather as heavy flooding regularly occurred, nor could it stand up to the ever increasing flow of wagon traffic.

Although Brampton was connected to the outside world by stagecoach, in particular the Brampton and Orangeville Stage Line, this often proved an unreliable method of transportation. What was needed was a railway line and, after many debates on the location, the Grand Trunk Railway, now known as the Canadian National

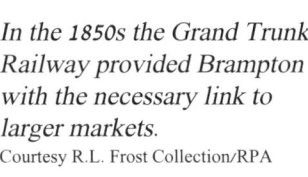

In the 1850s the Grand Trunk Railway provided Brampton with the necessary link to larger markets.
Courtesy R.L. Frost Collection/RPA

Railway or CNR, constructed a major line through the middle of the village. Situated just west of Main Street and south of Church Street, the train station opened in a blaze of glory on June 16, 1856. Farmers could now ship their agricultural produce to Toronto's main harbour in hours as opposed to days, and from there it could be shipped to every corner of the continent and the world. This greatly enhanced the infrastructure of the small village of Brampton and it quickly became a desirable location for opportunists.

Agriculture, Business and Manufacturing

The rich farmland of the Peel Plain surrounding the village brought early success in the wheat trade and thus enticed many merchants and mechanics to settle in the village, tripling the population over the

next five years. Before too long, Brampton boasted a brewery, a blacksmith, a saddlery, a tannery and several taverns and also attracted lawyers, doctors, pharmacists and other professionals to the town. The methods used in farming had grown in sophistication, and agriculture soon became the major industry for the surrounding area. In 1853, local farmers joined together to form the County of Peel Agricultural Society which gave them a forum for keeping up with the latest developments in breeding livestock and growing crops. The Haggert Brothers Foundry opened for business as a farm equipment manufacturer and provided employment to those not

In the 1860s, Brampton merchant, William Hurst, sold a wide variety of consumer goods in his general store located on Queen Street East.
Courtesy RPA

directly involved in the agricultural business. The company turned out some of the finest machinery in the land, including steam engines and boilers, harvesters and self rakes, reapers, mowers, sowers, feed mills and the Credit Valley Stove.

The four story Haggert Brothers Foundry, located at the corner of Main and Nelson streets employed many early Bramptonians. This view is looking south towards the "four corners," c. 1910. Courtesy R.L. Frost Collection/RPA

Brampton in 1863 was well on its way to becoming a Town. It had an established service and manufacturing industry with a core of forward-thinking leaders, who were filled with entrepreneurial spirit. Railway and telegraph offices were located in the centre of the village, connecting it to the outside world, and surrounding the core village was a well-established farming community, whose main crop, wheat, was highly marketable on the world stage.

The Dales Arrive in Brampton

It was to this environment that Edward brought his young family. With his experience in market gardening it was a natural choice, as the topography around Brampton was similar to Dorking insofar as the harsh Canadian winters would be tempered by the closeness of Lake Ontario, optimizing growing conditions for vegetables. Small plots of soil-rich land were readily available at reasonable prices and the air was clear and clean without the miasma of contagion found in England. Canada was free from the threat of continued involvement in European wars and Brampton offered a sense of stability for raising a family and starting a business. Seven established churches, from every denomination served the local population, which consisted mainly of English, Irish and Scottish heritage. There were good schools for Edward's children and an atmosphere of prosperity was in the air.

On June 26, 1863, the Dale family finally reached their destination and stepped off the Grand Trunk Railway at the Brampton Station. Edward was 36; his wife Sarah Warren was 33; and in tow was their twelve-year-old son Harry and their daughters, Sarah who was five, Ann who was three and baby Clara who was just three days shy of her first birthday. It is not recorded where they spent their first few nights and days but Brampton boasted several fine hotels at this time. It is a fair guess that until they could purchase a place to live they would have stayed in such an establishment as the Queen's Hotel or any of the boarding establishments that dotted the streets of Main and Queen in the village. Edward realized that the surrounding land was extremely fertile, could be easily leased and eventually would be available for him to purchase at a reasonable price. The Toronto market, like the London one he knew, was

Located on Queen Street East since the latter part of the 19th century, the Queen's Hotel was one of Brampton's earliest and finest hotels, c. 1900. Courtesy RPA

Brampton boasted many fine hotels and boarding establishments such as the Victoria House located on the main street of the village, c. 1890. Courtesy RPA

readily accessible via the excellent railway system of the Grand Trunk Railway and Edward Dale knew how to grow vegetables. He knew hard work. He had a son who was nearly of working age to help him and so the seeds for a future business opportunity and comfortable lifestyle were sown.

Notes:

1. 1861 Census, England; Internet Document
2. Internet document

Chapter 2

Settling in Brampton

1863 — 1876

Noteworthy Events of the Time

1865 American Civil War ends

1867 Dominion of Canada formed with BNA Act

1867 Brampton becomes the County Seat

1868 Brampton proposes incorporation as a Town

1868 Spanish Civil War

1869 Opening of the Suez Canal/Red River Rebellion

1873 Brampton officially incorporated as a Town

Over the next seven years, Edward worked diligently, establishing a market gardening operation with the help of his son Harry. On October 12, 1869 he purchased three and one-quarter

The original Hurontario trail which had traversed Brampton from the time of early settlement was called Main Street and was lined with lovely Maple trees, c. 1910.
Courtesy R.L. Frost Collection/RPA

acres at the northeast corner of Main and Vodden streets from William Ferguson for the sum of $900.[1] Part of the original Vodden farm, the property was ideally located for possible future expansion of the market gardening business. For the young family, life in Brampton in the last half of the 1800s was a welcome change from the oppressive atmosphere of England. The schools were free and both Harry and Sarah probably were enrolled at the new Central Public

St. Andrew's Presbyterian Church was built at its present location of Church and Alexander streets, c.1885.
Courtesy Waddell Collection/RPA

Settling in Brampton   9

School on Alexander Street. The family, registered as Church of England adherents in the 1871 census, most likely worshipped at the newly-built Christ Church on Joseph Street. In later years family members became affiliated with the Methodist and Presbyterian congregations — Grace United Church and St. Andrews Presbyterian. A very social family, they actively participated in all of the amenities that village life afforded, joining in the Annual Fall Fairs, village picnics, sporting events such as curling and lawn bowling, travelling concerts and other entertainments, all of which made up a highly-enriched lifestyle for the Dale family. In 1867, Canada declared itself a nation and the following year Brampton began the five year process to incorporate itself as a Town.

From its earliest days, Brampton provided lively social entertainments such as this firemen's demonstration and parade, c.1910. Courtesy R.L. Frost Collection/RPA

Market Gardening Enterprise

The infrastructure for agricultural mass production and shipment to the American and European markets was solidly in place, with wheat, cattle and pigs being shipped daily to the Toronto terminals from the farms of Peel County. These local farmers were mainly in the business of large-scale agricultural production and when they came to the village on the weekends for their home supplies, they sought additional fresh vegetables for their personal use.

It was into this niche that Edward sold his first crops of potatoes, cabbages, cauliflower and asparagus. His expertise as a market gardener gleaned from his years in Dorking, coupled with the rich

Wagons loaded with vegetables were driven from the Dale market gardening business to the trains for delivery to the large Toronto market, c. 1880. Courtesy RPA

soil of the Peel Plain, proved a winning combination and Edward's market gardening enterprise provided a decent living for his young family. Not only did he sell to the farmers on the weekends, he also peddled his produce door-to-door to the growing village population. Soon, as his business expanded, additional vegetables were grown and transported via wagon to the Grand Trunk Railway Station and on to the larger Toronto market.

First Greenhouse Operation

The Dales were a personable family blessed with good looks and a cheery disposition and thus Edward was a popular and welcome addition to the growing Brampton village. Sarah became pregnant within the year of their arrival in Canada and in January 1864 delivered another girl, Amy. Edward's business continued to grow and soon celery, radishes and lettuce were introduced to his established line of vegetables. These latter crops, unlike in the more temperate English climate, required hothouse production in Canada, and Edward built his first greenhouse, a dug out type, approximately 12 feet wide and 40 feet long, banked on the sides with clay and sod. It is reported that Edward hired a local carpenter named Mundy to build the greenhouse but this cannot be substantiated.[2] The heating for this initial hothouse was done by a flue furnace, which needed frequent feeding with extra logs at intervals throughout the night, particularly in the cold Canadian winters.

His son Harry, now 14, left school and began to work alongside his father in the fields and in the greenhouse. Young Harry proved to be a quick study and soon absorbed the accumulated knowledge of horticulture passed down from generations of Dale gardeners. Three years after their arrival, in the fall of 1866, Sarah gave birth to Edward Jr., a welcomed second son to help in the business. In the next four years Edward expanded and consolidated his market gardening enterprise by accumulating land in the north end of the village and moving in to their first home. As well, in March 1869, another daughter, Mary, was added to the growing Dale clan.

The Dale Rose

In the spring of 1870, when Harry turned 19, it became obvious to both father and son that Harry had inherited the Dale "green thumb" and a knack and abiding love for growing plants. In particular, the delicately-scented rose enthralled Harry. Where the original Dale rose that so fascinated Harry came from is not known for certain. It is reported that Edward was sent a root of the then popular "Marechal Niel," a rose that had been hybridized in 1864 by Pradel. At this time in Victorian England, many growers were involved in producing and propagating new species of roses. From wherever the original rose bush came, it is a widely held family story that there was an old rose bush that grew along the inner wall of the greenhouse that housed the vegetables. Harry, with the enthusiasm and ingenuity typical of truly great men, experimented with the shrub rose, cultivated it carefully and propagated it into a hot

The Dale Rose became a symbol for excellence and quality across the continent with over 500,000 roses shipped in the year 1890.
Courtesy Dale O'Hara Collection

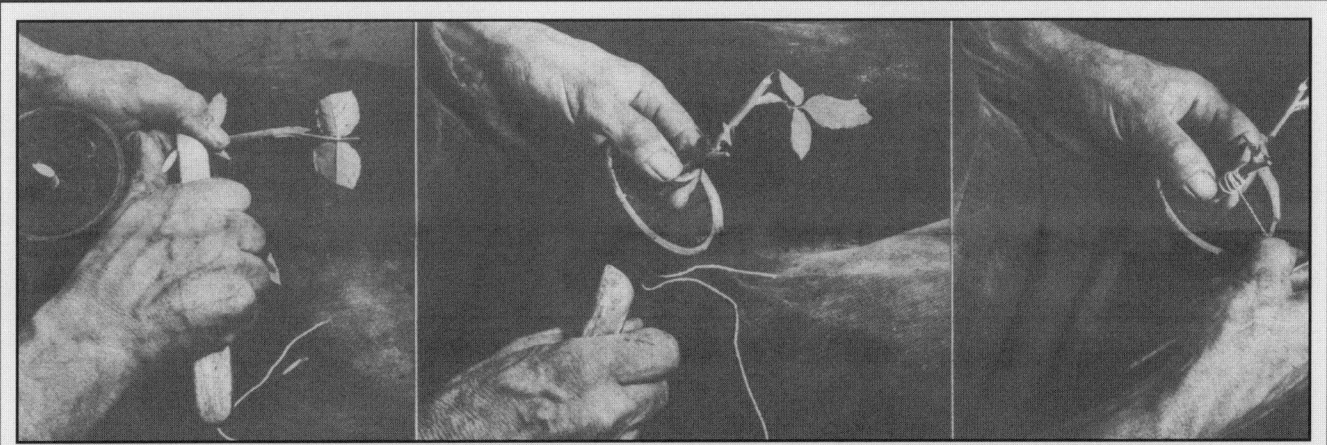

Grafting Roses

Grafting of a rose scion onto a Manetti plant was a skill perfected by the employees of Dales. Grafting involves inserting a piece of tissue from a desired rose into the trunk of a hardier rootstock. The roots of the hardier plant provide the nutrients and the energy to the desired rose and eventually the two fuse together. The roses that Harry grafted onto the vigorous rootstock grew faster and became larger plants more quickly than those very same roses grown on their own roots.

Courtesy R.K. Cooper Collection/RPA

house Hybrid Tea Rose. Harry had no formal training in floriculture, just what he had learned from his father, but through experimentation, he successfully produced marketable cut roses that were hardy, with sturdy stems and of excellent quality. Eventually Harry learned to graft his roses, which was not necessarily difficult, but required skill and some forethought before making the attempt.

With the advantages associated with grafted roses, Harry was able to produce cut roses year round of uniform size and colour, as well as uniform bloom size and shape. Harry discovered a rose root system that worked well in the growing conditions of his father's greenhouse and then he proceeded to choose the roses he preferred and continued to graft them onto the well-adapted roots. This gave him the opportunity to grow just about any rose type he wanted. Harry gradually honed this skill, becoming an expert in the grafting procedure and was thus able to selectively grow a multitude of different roses, all of high quality.

Family, Business and Town Thrive

In the 1871 Census[3], the family was listed as owning three and one-quarter acres of land, three acres devoted to garden, one of which was potatoes and one was in hay, the remainder in various

"Brampton possesses churches of every denomination and clergymen of every creed; schools and teachers of high repute; physicians of skill, who complain however of the unprofitable health sustaining salubrity of the place; bakers and butchers whose resources are taxed to their utmost extent to satisfy the demands of ever-increasing consumption; a Mechanics Institute, Reading Room and Lectares, a Miniature Theatre and Amateur Theatricals, Shoemakers and Dealers without number, a Foundry and Machine Shop and a large Flour Mill. We recommend to travelers on their way to the West, to stop and take up their abode for a few days in one of our economical hotels for a temporary sojourn in this delightful neighbourhood where so much goodwill and hospitality await them and where they may be tempted to secure permanent rest and a happy home. The place can boast also a number of very handsome and stately residences which would grace the neighbourhood of any city, and others are projected, which we are led to expect will be equally attractive. Added to these, we have a number of exceedingly commodious and well conducted hotels, where hospitality is dispensed with a liberal hand at moderate cost."

Since the 1870s, the Royal Hotel was one of Brampton's fine hotels. Courtesy R.L. Frost Collection/RPA

vegetables. They also owned one milk cow, three horned cattle, two pigs and sixty pounds of butter. In July that same year their eighth child, Thomas, was born, followed two years later by another son, William, completing the Edward Dale family. Edward was 46, Sarah 43, Harry, the eldest was 22 and William the baby, was just six months as the year 1873 began. Not only was Edward's family and business thriving just ten years after their arrival, so too was Brampton.

The first Town election was held in January 1874 for its 2,718 inhabitants. Numerous enterprises had been established, such as J.W. Cole, noted Brampton photographer who had a studio on the main street; the first Chief Constable was hired; seven churches, two banks, two telegraph offices, five good hotels and several general stores were in operation. Over 494 students attended the four public schools with 50 students, including the younger Dale

Brampton's earliest school, Central Grammar and Public School, built in 1856, was located at the corner of Alexander and Union streets. It housed both senior and junior students who were taught grammar, geography and British history, as well as the 3R's, c. 1900.
Courtesy R.L. Frost Collection/RPA

The Main Street studio of Brampton photographer J.W. Cole was fronted by wooden sidewalks with hitching posts for horses, c. 1870. Courtesy RPA

John Clarke's store occupied the northeast corner of Main and Queen, which is now the courtyard entrance to The Rose Theatre, c. 1890. Courtesy *Brampton 100th Anniversary Book/RPA*

"Haggertlea," built by John Haggert at the corner of Elizabeth, Nelson and George streets, boasted grape arbours, a fountain and a large terraced lawn. The house was later converted to apartments and can still be seen today, c. 1870. Courtesy RPA

The Dominion Building on Queen Street East housed Brampton's post office and government offices. This beautiful building is a city landmark, c.1910.
Courtesy R.L. Frost Collection/RPA

children, registered at Central Public School. Haggert Brothers, the iron and metal foundry, employed 140 people and had an annual payroll of $60,000. Brampton had become a thriving small town with all of the amenities necessary for success.

A Company is Born

In 1874 Edward and Harry entered a formal partnership and Harry started to take a more direct role in the family enterprise. Registered with the Province of Ontario, the agreement stated: *"We the undersigned agreed on the 12th day of February 1874 to enter into a Partnership as Market Gardeners and dealers in Garden and other Produce dividing profits of the business into three equal shares two of which shall be taken by Edward Dale and one by Henry Dale we contributing to the losses in like proportion. The business to be carried on under the name of Edward Dale and Son at the place occupied by us on Hurontario Street, Brampton. The term of partnership to continue so long as we so mutually agree. Dated Brampton 13 Dec. 1876. Witnessed by Robert Blair, registered by Wm. Duggan and signed by Edward Dale and Henry Dale."*[4]

Such was Harry's increasing interest in the growing of flowers, that he soon persuaded his father to add the sale of flowers to their burgeoning market gardening business. Again family lore tells the tale of Harry Dale peddling the family's vegetables door-to-door in the town of Brampton. Young Harry would take the time to stop and chat and, being so proud of his rose growing endeavour, he would present the lady of the house with one of his roses, requesting that she admire the beauty of its deep red colour and its fragrant perfume. Harry was a handsome young bachelor with the Dale charm and charisma and soon his customers began to request the roses as well as the fresh vegetables and the sale of flowers was begun in earnest.

It was apparent that Edward had made an excellent choice in Brampton as his destination, establishing the roots of what would eventually become the largest greenhouse operation in the world.

Notes:

---

1. Abstract Index to Deeds; RPA
2. The Wm. P. Bull Collection; RPA
3. 1871 Census; RPA
4. Archives of Ontario

Chapter 3

Formation of the Family Business
1876 — 1885

For the next nine years, Edward and Harry Dale, along with the younger members of the family, worked industriously in their market gardening business, accumulating land to grow their vegetables and gradually adding additional greenhouses. In 1875, by purchasing 50 acres of farmland north of their current properties from William Brody, Edward greatly increased their capacity for growing vegetables, both in the field and the greenhouses, as well as enabling them to increase the yield of cut flowers.

Harry Dale's Dynasty Begins

It was also the time that young Harry started his own dynasty. In 1878 at the age of 27, he married Elizabeth Young, a young Brampton woman whose family lived just a few streets away from the Dales. Bessie, as she was known, came from sturdy Irish stock, the eldest of six children of James Young and Jane Wright. Soon after their marriage, Harry and Bessie moved from the Dale family home on the northeast corner of Vodden and Main streets to their own home, a small house near the corner of Murray and Archibald streets. Their first child, Bertha, was born in 1879, followed by another daughter, Sarah, in 1881. Bessie proved to be an excellent addition to the Dale clan, contributing to the growing family business by adding a cherished Young family recipe of homemade pickles to the variety of produce sold by Edward and Harry.

Bessie and Harry Dale on their wedding day, 1878.
Courtesy Dale O'Hara Collection

Harry's passion, however, was not the market gardening of his father but rather growing roses, as he sought to not only sell them, but also to have the best roses in the wider florist trade. In order to do this, packing and shipping presented severe obstacles. The flowers needed to be packed in ice, surrounded by newspaper and shipped by rail in wooden boxes, with the timing of having the blooms in the correct stage of development needing to be absolutely perfect. The skill that this required became Harry's life, leading to even greater expansion of the greenhouses and between 1880 and 1885 two more greenhouses were added along the Main Street properties allowing for production of even more flowers. Harry it appears was not so much in the floral business for the money, although that certainly came with his success, as for the joy of producing finer and better flowers. All of this dedication paid off for him and at the New York City Exhibition in 1880, Dale roses captured the highest award.

Employees, such as these men, were dedicated to Harry Dale and their craft of producing the finest roses. (l to r) Len Suggit, Harry Dressel and J.B. Smith, c.1900. Courtesy Darren Spindler Collection

Greenhouses

At this time, the greenhouses were still mainly built in the same fashion as the original one with a couple of concrete steps at either end leading down to the dirt floor, three raised flower beds stretching the length of the house, and accessed by narrow walkways beneath the benches. Bales of straw were heaped around the foundations for insulation in the winter with manual vents opened and closed by hand in the warmer months.

It was during this time of expansion that the Fendley clan began to be intertwined with that of the Dales. James Fendley, a market gardener whose farm was on the 3rd line east of Brampton, had developed quite the "green thumb" for growing vegetables and flowers during the early 1870s. He peddled his wares from the back of his horse-drawn wagon along the concession roads outside Brampton, eventually moving his business into town. His son William Fendley became part of the Dale extended family by marrying Harry's 18-year-old sister, the lovely Amy Dale. After several years of marriage, following in the footsteps of both his father and his brother-in-law Harry, William decided to enter the trade and he started a substantial Fendley floral business. He gradually acquired land between Murray, English and Archibald streets at the north end of the town near the Dale properties, filling the niche vacated by Harry for market gardening and adding greenhouses which specialized in violets and carnations. In later years part of this land as well as all of the business was sold to the Dales.

Electricity, Water, Telegraph and Telephones

It was also during this period that many of Brampton's industries and Town municipal services began. As the population grew to 2,973, a 2200-volt line from the Hutton Power Plant in Huttonville brought electricity to the town. Brampton Waterworks was formed bringing a pipeline from nearby Snell's Lake to provide fresh water. There was a telegraph office run by P.L. Wood and in 1884 Brampton began its first telephone system, which was operated from the jewelry store of Algernon Williams, with a total of 23 subscribers. Brampton boasted the establishment of fine hotels, sporting clubs, general stores and businesses such as Stork's Pharmacy, Blain's Hardware and Charters Publishing Company, as well as the presence of a number of doctors, veterinarians, lawyers, teachers and ministers.

The arrival of electricity, water and telephone service in 1885 necessitated the re-construction of Brampton's main roads, such as Queen Street East. The Queen's Hotel and the Dominion Building are shown in the background, c. 1890. Courtesy *Brampton 100th Anniversary Book/RPA*

All of this greatly aided Harry in his growing operation. Although he had been able to irrigate his market gardening business with sufficient water from the Etobicoke Creek, it was now possible to provide his beloved roses with a reliable supply of fresh water from the town pipeline. As well, electricity provided a fairly consistent source of light which was needed by the plants in the dark winter months as well as for the optimum forcing of blooms. Harry's daughter Sarah,

A popular cut flower crop for Dales was the hardy chrysanthemum that Harry boasted came from "good, strong, healthy young stock," c.1898.

Courtesy Paul Willoughby Collection

in her later years recalled that in the early days of the business the electricity was only available during the daytime hours, so that many a winter night she and her father would go out into the pitch dark greenhouses with kerosene lanterns to close the vents and tend the fires. *"I can still hear the rattle of the panes and the whistle of the wind as we pulled on the chains or took down the little arms that held up the vents."*[1] The business of growing flowers, although producing a pleasant product, was extremely hard work. With the aid of the new telephone and telegraph systems, Harry could expand and efficiently run a continent-wide business. The increase in many town businesses attracted more people and hence augmented the available labour pool, which Harry required to operate his fields and his greenhouses. The volume of business continued to expand, and Edward Dale and Son began to enjoy an international reputation for growing fine quality flowers.

A Family Enterprise

With this international recognition of Harry's skill, it became apparent to Edward that Harry wanted to take the market gardening business

Aerial view of Edward Dale's home on the northeast corner of Vodden and Main streets, c. 1935. Courtesy *Brampton Now and Then* / L. Salisbury; photograph by Tommy Thomson

Harry's former frame house was eventually moved to form the shipping room, part of Dale's office complex, c. 1895. Courtesy Darren Spindler Collection

of Edward Dale and Son in a different direction and so, after a lifetime of hard work, Edward retired, passing on the management of the business to Harry. In 1880 Edward sold his 50 acres of farmland to E. Martin, and purchased a home for himself and his family on Rosedale Avenue. His property at the northeast corner of Vodden and Main, his remaining market gardening acreage, as well as all of the greenhouses were sold to Harry in 1882 and the partnership of Edward Dale and Son was dissolved. Harry became the driving force behind what was now referred to as Harry Dale, Florist. Harry moved his young family from Murray Street to the family home on Main Street in order to be closer to the greenhouses, which he continued to expand.

After the retirement of his father, Harry's younger brothers, Will, Ned and Tom, took a more active role in the production end of the business. With the expansion, Harry found less time to take part in the minute daily details required to run a rapidly expanding enterprise. Although the brothers did not share in the management of the company, Harry relied upon them to form a winning business combination. Harry was the visionary. Eventually, Ned took a leadership role, learning all aspects of the growing end of the business. Tom was more interested in the plant management from an engineering viewpoint, and Will, like Harry, became directly involved in growing the roses.

"Dales Flower Growers Brampton." Before boarding the train on this company outing to
a flower show, the employees gathered for a group photograph, *c.1900.*
Courtesy Darren Spindler Collection

Bessie was pregnant again in 1883 and another girl, Suzie, was
born and then, much to Harry and Bessie's delight, a son and heir,
Edward Henry Dale, was born on February 14, 1885. Harry Dale,
Florist, was making his mark upon the Canadian landscape. His
beloved roses were much sought after across the country and were
becoming known internationally as "Canada Roses."

Notes

---

1. *Growers Canada Magazine*; Dale O'Hara Collection

Chapter 4

King of Canadian Florists

1885 — 1900

Noteworthy Events of the Time

1893 *Toronto Star* first published

1894 First Stanley Cup awarded

1896 Modern Olympics begin in Athens, Greece

1896 Klondike Gold Rush

1897 Canada's first gasoline car

1899 Boer War in South Africa

1899 Spanish Civil War

W ith Harry now fully in charge, the company known simply as Harry Dale, Florist experienced a period of great growth. In Brampton as in most of Canada at this time, entrepreneurs were rewarded for their optimism, their audacity, their vision and their hard work. Not only were Harry's brothers involved in the business but his young children were also pressed into service.

In an interview with Harry's daughter Sarah, she described how she and her siblings were, from an early age, a part of the business. *"My earliest recollection is that of helping to weed the greenhouse beds. That was a job even the small children could easily do and all of the family worked in those days. They used ground benches and youngsters were closer to the work. There was always weeding in the fields in the summer for the largest part of the greenhouse business in the town of Brampton was still for vegetables. Market gardens covered the fields, and vegetables for the early market in Toronto were the backbone of the local horticultural trade. Asparagus beds stretched to the Etobicoke Creek with flower crops a rather small item."* [1]

A view of the Dale greenhouses looking west from the Etobicoke Creek where the annual cut of 500,000 roses was grown, c. 1900. Courtesy RPA

In 1887, Bessie bore twin daughters, Kate and Fan, bringing the family total to six children. By all early accounts, the business grew as rapidly as the family, with additional greenhouses being built or, in some cases, lengthened on a yearly basis. Although full of confidence as a young entrepreneur, Harry experienced a sobering moment in 1888 when his young daughter, Suzie, contracted measles that manifested itself initially as a late winter cold. Because of the lack of modern vaccination and medicine, five-year old Suzie died, as did many other children at the time. Bessie and Harry barely had time to mourn their loss as a multitude of tasks occupied their thoughts. Looking after their other children, including the twins, running the large household, expanding the business and entertaining the many visitors and guests who had come to view the greenhouses and Harry's magnificent flowers, consumed their everyday lives.

More Greenhouses, Houses and Family

By the year 1890 Harry was on the map as a grower of note, with numerous newspaper articles popping up throughout the continent extolling the wonder of the "glass houses in Brampton." In 1891 he won the Lenox Lyceum Prize for the Best Table of Roses at a flower show in New York. A congratulatory telegram reached Harry from the Lyceum, and it was said that he valued this written recognition

Dale employees constructed many of the early greenhouses, c. 1890. Courtesy Calvert Collection/RPA

as highly as he did the silver cup that accompanied it. From this time on, the development of the business was continuous. The greenhouses were extended in length from 100 to 350 feet to total 17,000 square feet of glass with the annual cut of roses in 1891 being 500,000 blooms. During the four succeeding years, four more greenhouses were erected prompting Bramptonians, who now numbered 3,000,

to make pilgrimages to the northern edges of the town at Main and Vodden streets in order to see these phenomenal houses *"with much talk being made about the incredible length of them."*[2]

Harry once again demonstrated his genius and his commitment to producing flowers of such high quality. Key to this success was in the actual greenhouse construction. His houses were erected in such a way as to ensure that cross braces and supporting beams cast no shadow, and all of the houses were situated to optimize the light in all seasons. Without proper greenhouse construction, the quality and quantity of flowers that Harry produced would not have been possible. Most of the greenhouses at this time were built on site by his own employees and then in later years by the well known company of Lord and Burnham.[3]

Many of the newer greenhouses were constructed by Lord and Burnham Co. Ltd.
Courtesy Special Collections/Toronto Reference Library

It was also during this period that Harry's business was profitable enough for him to build a larger house. This lovely mansion was erected in 1890 at the corner of Vodden and Main, on the opposite corner to the former Dale home.

A later view of the Harry Dale home and the vast acreage of greenhouses, c. *1920.* Courtesy RPA

Typical of houses built in Brampton at that time, it boasted a red brick exterior, beautiful stained glass windows, a wrap-around porch, front stairs, and back stairs for servants, a beautiful circular driveway edged with flower beds and it was snuggled right next to his beloved greenhouses.

In 1893, Bessie gave birth to her last child, Ethel, which would complete the Harry Dale family — Bertha, Sarah, Edward, Fan, Kate and Ethel.

Financial Problems

By 1895 Harry had seven greenhouses as well as an extensive market gardening operation. With his increased business in the growing and selling of cut flowers, mainly his much-prized roses,

This northeast view shows the extent of the greenhouses in 1895. Harry's wonderful mansion is nestled among his greenhouses on the southeast corner of Vodden and Main.
Courtesy Darren Spindler Collection

Harry realized he needed to expand, and in order to do this, he required loans which he thought would be readily available from the local banking establishments. He was dismayed to find that when he asked for a rating that the financial agency he approached would not give it, and he found that his business, seemingly so prosperous, was actually insolvent. Harry's strong suit had never been the accounting details required for the business but rather he had been more focused on his roses. He was a genius in his field, plugging away for the love of his craft rather than for the financial gain. This absence of detailed accounting made an investigation of the actual financial health of the firm difficult and consequently borrowing from any of the banks in the town was out of the question. Not a single loan company in Brampton was willing to take the risk.

Enter Thomas W. Duggan

The financial agency suggested that someone with knowledge of the fundamentals of business should be engaged to take charge of the financial end of things and they recommended Thomas W. Duggan.

Tommy, who was ten years younger than Harry, had paid his dues in the small village. Leaving school at the age of 14, he had worked in sales, and then as deputy sheriff of the county acting in the capacity of secretary to the county bench. Tommy Duggan was the polar opposite of Harry. His was a work ethic epitomized by a puritanical outlook, his philosophy being that pleasure was not allowed to interfere with business. His pious attention to religious duty, as a pillar of the Methodist community, and his rigid temperance outlook was the flip side to Harry's fun loving, easygoing, full-blooded approach to life, love and religion. Harry's single-minded vision was to produce roses, to make them finer and to grow more of them.

When approached by Harry, Tommy agreed to look at the books and at the end of his investigation, reported that if Harry's creditors decided to take concerted action, his affairs were in such bad shape that he would find himself in bankruptcy. Gone would be his business, his house and the livelihood of his 30 employees. Duggan agreed to take over the books and deal with all financial arrangements on the condition that he should be paid no salary until the end of the first year. At that time Harry was to decide what his new employee was worth to him. Harry had no choice and under these terms, he executed an unconditional power of attorney for his business affairs in favour of his new accountant, relinquishing control of the financial side of the business.

Portrait of T. W. Duggan, hired by Harry Dale as his accountant in 1895.
Courtesy RPA

Duggan immediately went to the banks and during that first year of his employment, 1895, was able to borrow from $15,000 to $20,000 in order to pay off the promissory notes that were owed for coal and other supplies. At the same time a vigorous campaign was instituted to change the practice for bill collection to a thirty-day basis. Harry, ever the bon vivant, had been allowing monies owed to the company to be left outstanding for approximately nine months. Harry feared that to press these customers for payment within thirty days would result in the loss of their business. This may well have been true in the early days, but Harry had failed to realize how much his business had grown in both prestige and power. Tommy also insisted that Harry write a Will and take out $15,000 of life insurance to cover the loans which had been obtained from the bank to pay off the various creditors. This move proved to be very fortuitous in the years ahead. In the beginning of their relationship it was clear that each man respected the talents of the other. Over the business of credit and bank loans, it is reputed that the conversation between Harry and Tommy went as follows: *"Look here Mr. Dale. I can't grow flowers and I don't interfere with you; you can't keep books so..."* The other saw the point. *"Tommy, you're right, but I'm scared. Do what you think best, but for heaven's sake don't tell me about it. I am a grower, a producer. I can make a success of my end of it but it needs a man like yourself for the business side to make Dale's Rose houses, a success."*[4]

The Dale greenhouses extended from the east side of Main Street, north to Vodden Street and east to the Etobicoke Creek. This view is westward towards Main Street along the extention of Victoria Terrace, c. 1900. Courtesy Darren Spindler Collection

Tommy Duggan assumed the position of accountant of the business on March 1, 1895. Armed now with capital, Harry over the next five years proceeded to expand his operation, adding square footage of greenhouses at an explosive rate. Statistics show that in 1896, with the population of Brampton standing at 3,070, the greenhouses expanded to 65,000 square feet of glass, comprising eight houses. The following year it was 90,000 square feet of glass, with an addition of three more houses. In 1898 another greenhouse was added, bringing the total to 125,000 square feet of glass and at the turn of the century there were 150,000 square feet of glass or approximately 15 to 20 greenhouses of varying lengths — more than double the size of just four years previously.

Harry's Interest in Floriculture

During these expansion years, Harry continued to take as much interest in the underlying scientific principles of floriculture as if he were an experimental station worker, making many trips to the United States to meet with other growers and thus improving his knowledge base of the floriculture of rose growing. In 1897 Harry returned from such a trip to be feted by his employees with what they called a jamboree at the Dale Conservatories. The affection his employees held for him was very apparent in the gift they presented him with — a wonderful carved armchair.[5]

Harry Dale grew a variety of high quality flowers in his greenhouses, including carnations, the so-called "poor man's rose," c.1898.
Courtesy Paul Willoughby Collection

In trade publications of the time, the high quality of Harry's stock was much in evidence. In 1898 George Stollery, a grower of carnations from Chicago, began a two-week tour of Canada and the United States visiting all of the leading rose and carnation growing establishments. After his trip, in a report to the Chicago Florists' Club he stated, *"An hour's ride from Toronto brought me to Mr. Dale's, Brampton, and here I saw the best roses I had ever seen. Brides and Maids, Perles and Hoste, were immense, flowers as large as Beauties and large quantities of them. The plants were very large and foliage like leather, making the finest example of health that one could wish."*[6]

In his trade book which Harry sent to potential customers he stated, *"After twenty years' experience in growing and selling cut flowers, such as roses, carnations, violets, chrysanthemums, mignonette, lily of the valley, etc. etc. during which time it has always been my aim to produce the very best goods possible, I think I can lay claim to having attained a front rank in the business. I am continually in receipt of testimonials from dealers both in Canada and United States as to the excellence of my stock. Having a large establishment (125,000 square feet of glass), I can generally be relied upon to fill all orders, and as I give my personal attention to the packing and shipping of same, they will be carefully packed with good flowers and forwarded promptly."*[7]

Brampton Becomes Sophisticated

Life was extremely good for the young Harry Dale family. Brampton moved from an agrarian society to an industrial and technological one. Organizations and services became more widespread and more sophisticated. The Fall Fair was established and held annually at its location on Wellington and Elliot streets. There were travelling circuses and menageries, theatre troupes and parades, live bands

Lawn bowling was a popular pastime in both public and private clubs for early Bramptonians, c. 1898. Courtesy RPA

and dances. Socially, Brampton was becoming quite sophisticated in its entertainment. The Dales were involved with their church, St. Andrew's Presbyterian on Church Street, with organized oyster suppers, strawberry festivals, garden parties and chicken suppers.

Harry was involved with the fledgling lacrosse team, the Excelsiors, which played with great success in the appropriately named Rosalea Park. This park, created on donated land from another market gardener and florist, Richard Jennings, was described as the best appearing and most beautiful park in Ontario. Torchlight parades and banquets greeted the Excelsior champions on a regular basis, and of course there were competitive teams in curling, ice hockey, rugby and baseball. There were private lawn bowling parties at Haggertlea, and public lawn bowling in Rosalea Park. Tennis, cricket, and cycling on a banked track, were also available for entertainment and participation.

The Dales frequently entertained visitors such as this group who had come to tour the greenhouses. Harry, unmistakable with his full beard and cap, is shown standing to the left in front of the pillar, while Bessie is seated in the middle, c.1898. Courtesy RPA

Harry's wonderful home on the southeast corner of Vodden and Main sat among his greenhouses with customers often being brought home for dinner in the midst of the brood of Dale children. A family story tells of Harry bringing customers to his home for dinner and on one such occasion his two little girls, Fan and Kate, begged their mother to take out her teeth, a party trick she did to amuse the children. Harry, by family accounts, was embarrassed but highly amused, for Bessie was known throughout the town as an extremely generous, fun loving woman, large in body as well as spirit. The Dale household was one of laughter and high spirits, one that never took life too seriously.

A Tragedy is Averted

Around this same time, Harry's youngest daughter Ethel, aged five, became quite ill with a chest infection. Bessie could not bear the thought of losing another daughter at such a young age and on the advice of doctors, boarded the train for warmer climates with her fragile daughter. Clara, Harry's sister, had married O.D. Matthews and moved to California several years earlier and welcomed the visitors to stay for the winter months with the hopes of giving Ethel a good chance to recover. Family recalled watching them board the train and thinking that they would never see young Ethel again; she was so ill. However, after several months, the baby of the family did recover and returned with her mother to Brampton much to the family's relief and delight.

An 1899 studio portrait of young Ethel Dale taken in San Diego, California.
Courtesy Dale O'Hara Collection

The Algies and the Dales

In 1897, the eldest Dale girls were approaching marriageable age and came to the attention of the Algie boys, William and James, who were heirs to the Algie Woolen Mill located in Alton. Riding down

Bertha Dale and William Algie Jr. on the veranda of the Dale home, June 2, 1899, their wedding day.
Courtesy RPA

from the Caledon Hills on horseback, they came courting and eventually won the hearts of Bertha and Sarah Dale. In 1899 Bertha married William Algie, moved to Alton and later back to Brampton into the sumptuous residence formerly owned by the Magills, which was located at Isabella and Archibald streets.

Sarah, who was two years younger than Bertha, was not in a rush to marry the fun loving James until some years later. She had taken a business course in Toronto at her father's insistence and was quite enjoying working alongside her father. *"The business was growing rapidly and the office work was beginning to get heavier every month so father and I decided that I should take a business course to learn the typewriter. That was something really daring in 1900 when only a few venturesome young women considered going into office work, which was still almost entirely a man's job. At Dale's I was the only female on the staff."* Harry was ahead of his time in recognizing Sarah's talents, sensing her keen mind and interest in all aspects of the business and she, in turn, was certainly a modern woman for the florist industry at the turn of the century was mostly a male-dominated profession.

Sarah Dale — the Modern Woman

By the time Sarah was 19, she was an integral part of the operation of the business. She was not only involved in the office but would also be called upon to help with the packing and shipping on the rush days. Orders mainly came in by telegraph or letter, for even though the telephone was in use by this time, it was considered a bit of a toy. Harry, ever the idea man looking for efficiency and increased production, had worked out a code whereby customers could order flowers by an alphabetical letter and number, via telegraph. Customers from as far away as Montreal, London and Quebec City could order speedily and accurately.

From her early years, Sarah Dale was involved in the family business, first as business manager and later as president of the company.
Courtesy Dale O'Hara Collection

In later years Sarah recalled, *"Our office did not have a type-writer. I did all the invoicing by hand. That is why I can recall so clearly the names of the florists and their shops in those days. We used to copy all the correspondence in longhand and put them into the big letterpress. Adding machines? We had never heard of them. We did not even have a time clock for the men working here. They would come to me at the end of the week and tell me how many hours they had put in working in the greenhouses or the fields or in the shipping room; then I would make up the pay. We had 40 to 50 men working in the plant, even in those days, and we had no night office staff. The telephone was installed in our house; we were among the first to make use of the new invention. Many a night, especially in holiday time have I been called out of bed to come downstairs by gaslight to take an order over the "phone." The orders were written on pieces of paper that were placed in a box at the side of the house. Early in the morning a young lad would come by to pick up the orders on his way to the shipping room so the flowers would be packed in time for the early morning train at seven o'clock. One of those young lads was W. A. (Bill) Beatty who in later years became president of the company. Bill, who was 13 years old at the time, earned 3 ½ cents an hour for working a 60 hour week."* [8]

The Century Comes to a Close

The century came to a close with Harry's business on a very firm foundation. Known across the continent as the "King of Canadian Florists," he regularly led tours through his greenhouses, and on one occasion personally conducted 50 florists from the United States through the expanse of glass. This large enterprise was the culmination of Harry's dream. For the past 15 years he had been feverishly expanding the greenhouses and mass producing his roses and flower stock. Now, he let it be known to his employees that he was content and was preparing to consolidate and concentrate on what he had, as opposed to more expansion.

In 1890 Main Street north was essentially rural with dirt roads fronting Harry's home and the greenhouses.
Courtesy R. K. Cooper Collection/RPA

On their daughter Bertha's wedding day in 1899, Harry Dale, his wife Bessie, the twins Fan and Kate and young Ethel stood for this family portrait among the wedding guests. Courtesy RPA

His eldest daughter was well married, his daughter Sarah was taking a keen interest in the business, his youngest daughter was once again healthy, and his cherished roses had gained an international reputation for excellence and quality. His phenomenal success was due to many factors — his innate ability and skill as a self-taught rosarian, his carefully constructed greenhouses, and his foresight in hiring Tommy Duggan and trusting his accounting skills. Through his charm, his dedication and natural leadership abilities, Harry knew how to instill loyalty and mutual respect in his employees.

This hard working, larger-than-life man was much loved by all, including his employees, as he made a habit of personally greeting each man as they arrived for work. A quote from a publication of the time describes Harry as, *"having the brains of a general. He knew his terrain, how to build his houses, how to heat them, and how to grow the flowers he loved. He knew his men too, with their strengths and weaknesses; where to place them, and how to get their best work."*[9]

It was said by those that knew him that Harry was a student of horticulture and a pioneer among successful rose growers, propagating and cultivating many varieties until the best the world had known was produced.

Notes

1. *Growers Canada Magazine*; Dale O'Hara Collection
2. *The Conservator*; RPA
3. Lord and Burnham Co. Ltd. *Handbook of Commercial Greenhouses and Materials 5th Edition 1926*; Toronto Reference Library AR 690.89029 L59.2
4. *Maclean's* Magazine; Brampton Library Archives
5. The Wm. P. Bull Collection; RPA
6. *The Conservator*; RPA
7. Darren Spindler Collection
8. *Growers Canada Magazine*; Dale O'Hara Collection
9. *Growers Canada Magazine*; Dale O'Hara Collection

Chapter 5

From Tragedy to Great Prosperity
1900 — 1915

Noteworthy Events of the Time

1901 Death of Queen Victoria

1902 First Transatlantic radio report

1909 Peary reaches the North Pole

1913 Immigration tops 400,870

1912 Sinking of the Titanic

1914 – 1918 World War I

T he 20th century began on an upswing in the economy with 1900 to 1910 being described as the greatest growth years in the history of the country. This period is often referred to as the "Wheat Boom" for the export of agricultural products dominated the growth and wealth of the nation. It brought with it an increase in immigration that peaked in 1913 and an increase in per capita output (GDP), reflecting a corresponding increase in the general welfare of the nation. Life in the young country of Canada was filled with great prosperity.

Tragedy Strikes

With business looking so promising for Harry Dale's company, tragedy struck. Brampton's daily newspaper, *The Conservator*, ran the following notice on January 5, 1900. "*Sudden and unexpected and somewhat startling was the announcement of the death of Mrs. Harry Dale on Wednesday morning at the age of 41 years. She had been ill only a short time and underwent an operation on Monday night, but the desired end was not attained. Mrs. Dale was a kind-hearted, cheerful woman, and made friends of those with whom she came in contact. She leaves a family of five daughters and one son, who with the grief stricken husband, have the heartfelt sympathy of a very wide circle of relatives and friends. The funeral this afternoon was very largely attended, service being conducted by Rev. W.C. Clark, pastor of the Presbyterian Church.*"[1]

Bessie had just returned from San Diego, California and was finally reunited with both husband and children after a long winter of separation. There is no record of the actual cause of death but at that time major surgery was only performed in Toronto. In all probability death was due to peritonitis after some type of abdominal perforation, possibly a bowel obstruction. Illness probably occurred rapidly but even with surgery, death was inevitable for modern antibiotics were not yet available. One can only speculate how bereft Harry felt. He had been happily married for 22 years and he and Bessie had built not only a highly successful and respected business, but also a wonderful family and lifestyle. The family was left without a mother to run the large household and manage the younger children, as the twins were twelve and Ethel, the baby of the family, was just six years old. Harry decided that Sarah, the eldest unmarried daughter, would take over the management of the Dale household and help to raise her brother and sisters. The family struggled through the crisis over the winter months, and the business continued unabated riding the crest of prosperous times.

Spring arrived and, perhaps because of the death of his wife, Harry realized that he needed to arrange for proper provision for his children and direction for the company in case anything should happen to him. In March 1900, he clarified his Will in the presence of his brother Ned, and a trusted employee Henry G. Mullis. Spring rolled into summer and just as Harry was beginning to get through the worst of the mourning period, the unthinkable happened. Harry Dale died a tragic and unfortunate death.

A Family and a Town Mourn

In late June 1900, Harry suffered a toothache requiring dental work, in all probability an extraction. Although contaminated dental tools are suspected, for whatever reason, Harry developed blood poisoning. With no modern antibiotics such as penicillin available, or a true understanding of the spread of disease, Harry's health gradually deteriorated over a two-week period beginning on the first of July. News of his illness, falling on the heels of his wife's death was reported in the Friday July 13, 1900 edition of *The Conservator*. *"The condition of Mr. Harry Dale, in which the whole town has taken a sincere interest from day to day during his illness, is of a very depressing character today. Little hope is now entertained of his recovery. But still while there is life there is hope, and tomorrow the family and friends may be rejoicing at the prospect of his life being spared."*

It was not to be and Harry died on Sunday July 15, 1900. On July 17, his obituary in *The Conservator* read, *"Harry Dale died on Sunday night from blood poisoning, after an illness of two weeks. No death has occurred in this municipality for years that has brought forth such general expressions of sorrow. Everybody knew Harry Dale. Everybody had the same opinion of his uprightness of character and the reliability of his methods. His knowledge of the business in which he was engaged and his enterprise in furthering that business were known throughout the length and breadth of the land. His death is a loss to his young family, who were left motherless just six months ago; a loss to his employees, who were deeply attached to him; and a loss to the town of Brampton which is deeply felt by her citizens. Six months ago Mrs. Dale died. The family consists of five daughters, the eldest being Mrs. Wm. Algie, Jr. of Alton, and one son, for whom the deepest sympathy is felt. The funeral this afternoon was largely attended. The service was conducted by Rev. Mr. Clark, of the Presbyterian Church. Floral tributes of most attractive designs were sent by his fellow florists on both sides of the line and by his employees and other friends."*

Harry Dale's Will

The Dale children were orphaned and the burgeoning business was left without its leader. There was great consternation among both those who ran the affairs of Brampton and the employees of the company as to what was going to happen. Almost one-quarter of the town's population relied on Harry Dale's company for employment, with many peripheral businesses dependent on its success. It was generally assumed that the operation would be sold or dismantled, for without Harry there were no flowers. Harry was the business. For all of his lack of financial expertise, Harry in the end proved why he was so successful, as he had the foresight to leave a business plan in his Will. Not only did he lay out the details for the provision of his young

A studio portrait of Harry Dale, the "King of Canadian Florists," c.1895. Courtesy Calvert Collection/RPA

family and his disabled sister Annie, but he also left a blueprint for the future of his company. At the reading of Harry's Will, Tommy Duggan and William Algie Sr., the father-in-law of Bertha Dale Algie, were named joint executors of Harry's estate as well as Duggan being named as guardian of the underage Dale children.

Harry Dale's Will stated that: *"My executors are empowered to dispose of part or all of my estate, real and personal, at any time they deem best but may in their discretion continue my business as Florist to a period not exceeding that, when my youngest surviving child, arrives at the age of twenty-one. During such continuance, my executors are to have full power to deal with the income derived therefrom in whatever way seems to them most advantageous to my estate. My life assurance money is to be used as far as necessary in liquidating claims against my estate. The balance (if any) of the life assurance money and all moneys derived from the sale or management of my estate not needed, in the opinion of my executors, for the purpose of carrying on my business as Florist, are to be invested in such securities as my executors shall choose."*[3]

A 1902 portrait of the Dale children: Front row (l to r) Sarah, Ted, Bertha. Back row (l to r) Fan, Ethel and Kate.
Courtesy Dale O'Hara Collection

Harry, ever the general, had laid out a viable, practical plan to take care of his children, as well as his employees. The $15,000 life insurance policy that Duggan had fortuitously persuaded Harry to take out five years previously provided sufficient working capital to enable the business to be wound up without losses.

T.W. Duggan Carries On

At this time, the Dale greenhouses were the largest on the North American continent and work was in progress for the erection of new buildings that would increase the greenhouse space to 250,000

New greenhouses or "ranges" began to be built at an accelerated rate increasing to 250,000 square feet of glass, c. 1910. Courtesy RPA

square feet of glass. Tommy Duggan, Harry's accountant and business confidant, had a clear mandate from Harry to carry on. T.W., as he was now known, had been with Harry for five years, was largely responsible for putting the business on a firm financial footing and could see its growth potential. Because he was not salaried but rather took a percentage of the yearly profit, Duggan was accumulating personal wealth and, therefore, it was in his best interest to continue the business and maintain his lucrative position. In a magazine interview in later years, Duggan was asked why he did not wind up Harry's estate. He replied, *"I gathered all the information I could, read everything I could lay my hands on, and the following year I made an extensive trip through England, France, Holland and Germany. As a result of my investigation I found that the flower industry there was as stable as the cloth industry. The facts were, that co-incident with the growth of the country, continuous expansion was justifiable. As the Dominion grew in population and wealth, it must grow in culture, and wealth and culture would demand flowers. So I borrowed from the banks and private individuals and expanded the plant."*[4]

Lord and Burnham Co. Ltd., specialists in greenhouse construction, were hired to raise many of the new greenhouses. Courtesy Special Collections/Toronto Reference Library

A Strong Work Ethic

Where Harry Dale was a genius when it came to growing roses and other flowers, T.W. was his equal in financial affairs. He knew how to turn a profit and how to maintain Harry's tremendous floral business.

However, he needed capital. As power of attorney for the business and executor of Harry's estate, T.W. Duggan borrowed $140,000 over a period of the next three years, much of it obtained in loans of $5,000 and $10,000 from long time friends and acquaintances in Brampton. Without the confidence of the folks of Brampton, that growth would not have been possible. He left the day-to-day running of the growing side of the business to Harry's brothers, Will, Ned, and Tom, and other loyal employees who had been with Harry from the beginning. All were extremely knowledgeable about how to continue with the production and quality for which Dales was famous.

A Tourist Attraction

In 1900 such was the reputation of the greenhouses that they became a tourist attraction, bringing the first motorcar to Brampton. Lord and Lady Minto drove their fancy new car to view the "marvellous houses of glass" of the Harry Dale "Conservatories" and to tour through the rows of roses and other fragrant blooms. Duggan and his children are shown standing at the rear of the automobile.
Courtesy Brampton 100th Anniversary Book/RPA

Duggan began his expansion. He took charge of the business and had himself appointed managing executor with his first task being to change the thirty-day credit requirement to just fifteen days. Harry would have been appalled at this move, but it made great business sense because when customers did not promptly pay the producer, it meant Dale's business was suffering. By making the business either COD or fifteen days credit, it ensured that the company had a solid cash base. His second task was to put into practice his marketing policy for he was of the belief that one did not wait for markets. With the advent of large-scale production, cut flowers came within the reach of the average person's purse, and the unit cost principle was put into effect. Everything they sold was based upon the actual cost of the production plus a reasonable profit. As a result of this policy an ever-widening market was created. Duggan was able to accomplish this by offering a good work environment, albeit with very low wages. In the early days, the business was run much like the military. The "lieutenants," as the managers were called, often worked their way up to leadership roles through the "ranks." The Dale employees were treated with the camaraderie of the military with clearly defined roles, expectations and rewards.

T.W. brought to the business some old-fashioned ideas, which are the basic principles of success in every business. He was an indefatigable worker who rarely, if ever, took a vacation. He had few outside interests, with his only hobby being his work. Although in his youth he was involved with the Brampton Lacrosse Club, he did not pursue the pleasures of Brampton society. He neither drank nor smoked, did not gamble or play sports, such as the popular town pastimes of golf and lawn bowling. He was described in a *MacLean's* magazine article as being, *"a kindly business man, keen and likeable, shrewd but unswervingly honest, sympathetic though not to be imposed upon."*[5] His early Primitive Methodist upbringing formed his character both personally and professionally.

The Dale children, Ted, Fan, Kate and young Ethel remained in the large Dale home as per Harry's Will, along with Sarah who acted as both mother and father. The rather dour, puritanical T.W. Duggan, acting as their legal guardian, kept a tight rein on the family finances. As Harry had stated in his Will, *"My executors are to pay out of the income from my estate to or for my children while they remain unmarried, in such sums and at such times as my executors consider proper, whatever moneys my executors deem necessary for their maintenance and education."*[6] All financial and personal requests by Harry's children had to be made to and judged worthy by their guardian, a situation that caused some animosity over the years.

The era of T.W. Duggan's management began.

Duke and Duchess of York Visit Brampton

In 1901, a bare year after Harry's death, the Duke and Duchess of York visited Canada making a stop in Brampton. A fitting reception for their Royal Highnesses was arranged at the Grand Trunk Railway Station. Thomas Thauburn, Mayor of Brampton, extended a formal welcome after being presented to the Duke and Duchess by Major Maude. Mr. Thauburn, in turn presented T.W. Duggan and William Algie Sr., executors of what was now referred to as the Harry Dale Estate, along with other prominent townspeople. Daughters and nieces of Harry Dale, T.W. Duggan and MP Blain presented magnificent bouquets of flowers to the Duchess. The Duke expressed his genuine pleasure and gratitude for so many beautiful flowers, with the Duchess being particularly enthusiastic

Young girls presented flowers to the Duke and Duchess of York on their visit in 1901. Standing on the steps of the Dale home, back row (l to r) Ethel, Kate, and Fan Dale, Phoebe Algie; middle row (l to r) Dorothy Duggan, Lillian and Bess Dale; front row Miriam Blain. On the left front is William Algie Sr., on the back left is Mrs. Blain and Mayor Thauburn is standing on the back right. Courtesy RPA

in her appreciation. In a newspaper account of the day, it was reported that the Duchess, speaking about the flowers, *"enquired if they were really grown here and being answered in the affirmative expressed regret that the arrangements which were made would not permit them to remain longer. The flowers were the finest they had seen on their tour."*[7] A photograph in the same newspaper showed the small girls with their large bouquets of diverse flowers arranged to demonstrate the quality of the blooms produced by Dales. One can only imagine those wee girls staggering under the weight of the floral arrangements as each of the bouquets had dozens of flowers as well as the designer tools of wire, baskets and sphagnum moss.

Marketing Abroad

In 1902, T.W. put his business and marketing plan into action. With his two sons Broddy and Charley, he set sail for Europe, in particular Germany and Holland, for two months, sailing on July 5 from New York and landing at Rotterdam in Holland. Rotterdam produced bulbs of superior quality and it was there that Duggan formed a business connection that would enable the Harry Dale Estate to make their large yearly imports directly from the original producers with additional profit going to the Estate. They proceeded to Hamburg, the home of the lily of the valley known and prized the world over as the favourite flower of Queen Alexandra. This flower grew from pips, three-quarters of a million of which were imported every year by the firm. These too, in future, would be received directly from the original cultivators.

T.W. mixed business with pleasure and toured Berlin, Potsdam and London, where he viewed the coronation of King Edward VII and Queen Mary, as well as visiting Scotland and Ireland. In Belfast, Harry had previously made a direct business agreement with the firm selling Manetta stocks, used as the rootstock for the roses and Duggan was able to consolidate and re-confirm this in person. In all the places that T.W. visited, he inspected the conservatories and greenhouses and in an interview upon his return in *The Conservator*, he declared, *"There are none to compare with our own in excellence of equipment and modern methods but there are some larger, one in England covering 30 acres. In no place in the United States or England do the men receive as good wages as are paid by the Dale Estate and I hope that conditions in the future may make it possible to maintain if not improve this gratifying state of affairs."*[8]

It was during this same trip that he met and persuaded Walter Calvert, a young highly-experienced grower from England, to immigrate to Canada and work for him. Walter jumped at the opportunity, arriving in Brampton in March 1905, and Ada, his fiancee, joined him the following year. Walter would eventually branch out on his own to form the Walter E. Calvert Company.

On Duggan's return, the employees assembled in the office, and presented him with a stunningly handsome oak chair. William Algie Sr. co-executor of the Dale Estate, as it was now known, read an extremely long-winded, flowery speech that re-capped Duggan's trip. The article concluded with, *"The people of Brampton join with Mr. Algie and the employees of the Dale Estate in welcoming home the man who has done so well for the business and in doing that, greatly benefited the whole municipality."*[9] It is no wonder that the safe return of Duggan was so appreciated. At that time, the Dale Estate employed upwards of 40 men, approximately one-quarter of the town's workforce. The people of Brampton recognized that Duggan was the only hope of keeping the Estate solvent, expanding and profitable and, where the fortunes of the Dale Estate went, so went theirs.

In 1908 the greenhouses were extended in both length and acreage filling the "flats" between Main Street and the Etobicoke Creek. Courtesy R. L. Frost Collection/RPA

The Dale Estate Puts Brampton on the Map

The business was increasing in capacity as well as in continental and worldwide reputation. Most publications at the time made note of the size of the greenhouses, running articles and photographs of their immensity. A newspaper article in 1903 aptly describes how the Estate was viewed in the world outside the small confines of Brampton, whose population at that time was just 3,150. C.W. Young, editor of the *Cornwall Freeholder,* paid a visit to Dale's greenhouses and the following article appeared in his paper February 20, 1903. *"Brampton, which is a small town of a few thousand inhabitants, may fairly claim pre-eminence in the matter of growing flowers under glass. This industry has been steadily growing for a dozen years or so, and now there are three large concerns in active operation — the most extensive of which is the Dale Estate, which has reduced the business to almost an exact science, and whose product sets the pace for quality in New York, Boston, and other American cities. The new greenhouses are not visible from the street, and on stepping out of the driving snow storm, nothing indicates what is to be seen further on, the eye taking in a huge storehouse with the capacity of several thousand tons of coal, a battery of boilers, all fed by automatic stokers, an engine and other appliances which would seem to have no connection whatever with a flower garden. But the opening of another door reveals a vista of beauty. The temperature is summer like and as far as they can reach, are roses in bloom. The carnations require a cooler temperature and the house for them is separate. A glass covered passageway connects the new and the old plant and is utilized for the growth of lily of the valley, the waxy whiteness of the thousands of blooms and the delicate petals being fairly enchanting. Roses and carnations fill up most of the old houses but there is in one, nearly an acre of violets and mignonette; another with hundreds of Easter Lilies just coming into bloom, still another with golden yellow daffodils and snow white hyacinths and still another with a perfect*

Daffodils in bloom stretched the length of the greenhouses, a breath of spring in the cold winter months. Courtesy Doug Fines

wilderness of greenery, smilax and asparagus fern. In the packing house, immense quantities of cut blooms are being packed for shipment to all parts of the continent, and perishable as they may seem to be, the methods are so perfect that absolute freshness is ensured even should their destination be Nova Scotia or California. New York especially admires Canada Roses. They attracted attention first by the many prizes captured by the Dale Estate, and later by the fact that they lasted longer than those grown in the US greenhouses. As one passes a florist's windows in any considerable American city, one sees Canada Roses advertised as the standard of quality. Where the golfers were driving their balls last summer, there are now 21 glass houses, three or four acres having recently been added to the already large plant. The new section devoted to carnations is about two acres in extent. There must be a couple of hundred men engaged in their fascinating employment of growing flowers and so far as appears, the business is capable of indefinite expansion as the taste for flowers is constantly increasing."[10]

The Introduction of Orchids

Part of the growth and popularity of the Dale Estate was due to the introduction of orchids to their stock in 1911. A Dane, who was employed by the Estate in forcing lily of the valley, had been accustomed to growing orchids in England and missed them.

Ten specialized greenhouses were constructed to house the production of the exotic orchids, c. 1910.
Courtesy Paul Willoughby Collection

Duggan decided to give this lover of orchids his chance, securing stock from Brazil. An experimental orchid house, 30 feet in length, was created on the south side of Rosedale Avenue East and, after two years of experimentation, it was found that the tropical flower could be grown in the northern temperate zone. Nine more houses were built, each 115 feet long, and by 1915 Dales had 60,000 orchid plants under cultivation. A newspaper article detailed a visit to the Estate undertaken specifically to see the orchids stating, *"such were their quality that A.C. Burrage, known as the 'Copper King' of the USA came to Brampton in his private car to visit the orchid house of the Dale Estate. Mr. Burrage makes a hobby of orchid growing and received much food for thought as he traversed the ten great orchid houses."[12]*

The Business and the Family Continue to Grow

At this time Harry's brothers were heavily involved with the growing end of the business and were a big part of its success. Sarah, his daughter, the only woman on staff, continued to work in the office until her marriage to James Algie in 1907. The brothers remained an integral part of Dales, with Edward (Ned) Dale holding the position of general superintendent, Tom Dale the head engineer, and Will Dale the foreman of the rose operation. H.G. Mullis was head of the outgoing shipping department; Tom Davis took the orders and the assistant manager to T.W. Duggan was J.E. Cooper.

In order to extend the expertise of the staff involved directly in the cultivation end of the business, more men from the United Kingdom, who were specialists in various fields such as roses, carnations, ferns, orchids and chrysanthemums, were hired. Fred Bacon recalls, *"My father, Charles Bacon, 'came out' in 1910 as a specialist in the propagation and growing of carnations, and he was the foreman of the entire carnation operation for his term of 50 years at Dale's. My father did not have a white-collar job, even though he was a foreman, but I never knew him to go to work without a collar and tie, and he never took it off, even on very hot days. He would work from 9 to 5 and 7 to 12 on Saturday but he also went in every Sunday morning, usually from 7 to 10. He did this for all of his 50 years at Dale's. I don't recall him ever having or taking a holiday. I imagine the white-collar folks got holidays, but not the men in the greenhouse. How could they? The plants demanded round the clock attention, all day, every day."*[13]

Vice Regal visitors toured the Dale Estate in July of 1908. (l to r) T.W. Duggan, Mayor Golding, H. Mulliss, Ned Dale, G. Williams, Capt. Newton ADC, Lady Parker, Her Excellency Countess Grey and J.E. Cooper. Courtesy Brampton 100th Anniversary Book/RPA

Over the course of the next 15 years, the business entered a period of unprecedented growth. Coupled with a conservative fiscal policy, a tightly managed business, a dedicated cadre of workers and a booming economy, the Dale Estate surpassed all expectations. From 150,000 square feet of glass greenhouses in 1899, it had expanded to 1,250,000 square feet under glass by 1913; from 40 employees in 1900, a workforce of 205 was registered on the payroll in 1915. Expansion accelerated, with approximately ten greenhouses being added per year. By 1915, the firm owned 127 acres of land of which 26 acres were under glass and the Dale Estate was known as having the third largest number of greenhouses in the world. Most of the employees were of British heritage bringing with them their love of gardens and flowers. In the greenhouses were grown a variety of cultivated flowers and bulbs such as carnations, chrysanthemums,

In 1906, the Shipping Room was the staging area for all of the cut flowers. Shown here are William Beatty to the left of the clock, Ned Dale in the foreground and T.W. Duggan on the right along with a number of other Dale employees. Courtesy RPA

violet plants, orchid plants, asparagus plants, sweet peas, ferns, mignonette, gladioli and, of course the world famous roses. Ever since their first triumph in New York in 1891, Dales continued to capture flower show prizes. In 1915 at the Cleveland Flower Show, they carried off three Firsts in Society Specials category, four Firsts in Colour Specials and a First in Pompous and Singles. Prize winning at local Ontario shows was so commonplace they were scarcely remarked upon.

While all of this tremendous growth in glass and flowers was unfolding, the Dale family grew up, married and moved out of the

A sample of the various medals won by the Dale Estate at flower shows in the USA and Canada.
Courtesy Virginia Gould Collection/Photographs by Finn O'Hara

family home. The men in the greenhouses fondly remembered Sarah, their one time office manager, and raised money to buy her a wedding present of a china cabinet that she proudly kept within her family throughout her remaining years. Fan and Kate, after being away at finishing school in Whitby for a year, soon left home for married life. Fan married William Beatty, who had started to work full-time at Dales, and they moved to a home on Market Street; Kate married Robert (Rab) Campbell, a glass blower, and moved into a company-owned house on the northeast corner of Main and Vodden.

Edward Dale Sr., the Englishman who took a chance in 1863 and brought his family to Canada, died quietly and without public fanfare in 1909 just nine short years after his son Harry. The business that he had started so humbly as a market gardening family operation had grown into a gigantic floral empire.

Young Edward (Ted) Dale, the son and heir to the Dale Estate, was expected to enter the business at this time and eventually take over the reins.

Ethel Dale, seated in front wearing a white blouse, and her cousins enjoy a summer afternoon at the Dale family home, c. 1910.
Courtesy Dale O'Hara Collection

Ted Dale Coming of Age

Duggan arranged for Ted to go to Toronto to take a business management course and young, handsome, man-about-town, Ted, discovered the joys and exciting nightlife of the big city. Upon his return, he was put to work at the bottom of the ladder, performing the lowest jobs of cleaning out the horse stalls and working in the greenhouses in order to learn the business from the ground up, much like his father and uncles had done. In all probability, Duggan was trying to groom young Ted to have an appreciation of all aspects of the business in order for him to make the leap to management. However, Ted had

A young Ted Dale with friends who were part of the Etobicoke Baseball Team pose for the camera. (l to r) Bob Campbell, Harry Campbell, Ken Stewart, Charlie Mullis, Ted Dale, Jim Stewart, Bill Beatty, Charlie Fendley, Ern Young and Bob Beatty, c. 1910.
Courtesy Dale O'Hara Collection

Ethel Dale (standing) and her cousin Bess Dale (middle) and a friend epitomize the joy of youth in 1913. Courtesy Dale O'Hara Collection

witnessed Harry's Will and knew that he was to take the majority share in the assets of Harry's estate and felt that the business was, to all intent and purposes, his. From family accounts, Ted was a bit on the wild side and quite spoiled and pampered by his sisters. He felt that it was unfair that he had to work as a labourer while Duggan's sons, who were of the same age, were given office jobs. In disgust, Ted quit work in the Dale Estate and never again worked a day in his life, holding positions in the company in name only.

Ethel Dale pictured on her graduation day from the Ontario Ladies College in Whitby, Ontario, c. 1913.

Courtesy Dale O'Hara Collection

He was described by family members as a "devil-may-care" type and a great prankster, with a dog he affectionately called "Old Ass." With considerable leisure time, Ted decided that he wanted to learn to play the piano and began to take lessons from Alice Robinson, of the respected and long time Brampton Hall-Robinson family. Although Alice was considerably older than young Ted she let it be known that she would one day marry the heir apparent to the Dale Estate, which she did when they eloped to Toronto on Valentine's Day in 1912. Ted and Alice took up residence on Johnson Avenue and then moved back to the Dale family home in 1914, when Ethel married at age 21.

A Profitable Living for All

Duggan still operated on a yearly share of the profit of the company. His hard work paid off handsomely and he enjoyed an enviable business and social reputation as a pillar of Brampton society. He built a magnificent mansion at the corner of Frederick and Main streets, continuing to walk to work and greet employees as they arrived in the morning and often being the last one to turn out the lights at night. Like Harry, he took a keen interest in all aspects of the business, but the growing end was still left to Harry's brothers and other long time employees.

T.W.Duggan built this luxurious mansion which still remains in its original state, at the corner of Frederick and Main streets. Courtesy RPA

Although all of the Dale women were married, only Fan's husband entered the family firm. Ethel had been courted by William Brydon for several years, but she had waited until she had reached the age of majority to marry, thus avoiding having to ask her strict guardian, T.W. Duggan, for permission to marry. Her husband Dr. William Brydon set up his medical practice alongside his uncle Dr. William Hall on the main street in Brampton. William and James Algie as well as Robert Campbell, husbands of the other Dale women, chose instead to live on the Estate income of their spouses, enjoying all that the social life in Brampton offered. Each of Harry's heirs received a monthly share of the company's profit with Duggan still keeping the reins of the business firmly in his hands. This allowed each of the Dale siblings and their spouses to enjoy a very comfortable lifestyle.

Photographed on the stairway landing of the family home is Ethel Dale on her wedding day, April 29, 1914. She is carrying an exquisite floral bouquet of the best pink roses that the Dale Estate produced.
Courtesy Dale O'Hara Collection

Standing at the entrance to the Dale Estate offices are two members of the Cooper family. This building eventually became almost completely covered with ivy and remained as pictured until the mid 1960s. The administrative offices are pictured on the right with the sales and shipping departments housed at the rear. Note the new construction of the greenhouse to the left of the building supplanting the former outdoor gardens.
Courtesy R.K. Cooper Collection/RPA

Harry's Dynasty Lives On

In 1914, with the youngest child, Ethel, reaching the age of 21, the last of Harry's directions for his company as stipulated in his Will, came into play. It stated that, *"When the youngest surviving child becomes twenty-one, I desire my executors to dispose of my estate Real and Personal, and wind up my estate."*[14] Little would Harry have believed that within 15 years of his death, his business had become the largest of its type in the world, with more than 205 employees dependent upon it for their livelihood.

There was a claim that the Dale Estate had outrageous profits and assets and received unfair considerations in the form of tax incentives from the Town. In reply T.W. Duggan wrote that, the majority of the buildings were constructed by their own employees during slack times when the men would normally have been laid off; loans could not be secured due to the high risk of the buildings and stock; large taxes to the Town were being paid; and Dales added continuously to their workforce at no cost to the Town. He concluded that their rapid expansion came at considerable cost and risk but

The Dale Estate continued to win honours at national and international flower shows. This magnificent silver cup was awarded for their roses at the second annual exhibition of the American Rose Society held in New York in March 1901.

Courtesy Dale O'Hara Collection,
Photograph by Finn O'Hara

that the company was willing to undertake this in order to build up a business that would bring in revenue and be a credit to the Town.[15]

The Dale Estate was both admired and envied for their phenomenal worldwide success and reputation. There was no way that Duggan would allow such an enterprise to be dismantled and liquidated.

Notes

1. *The Conservator*; RPA
2. The Wm. P. Bull Collection; RPA
3. The Wm. P. Bull Collection; RPA
4. *MacLean's* Magazine; Brampton Library Archives
5. *MacLean's* Magazine; Brampton Library Archives
6. The Wm. P. Bull Collection; RPA
7. *The Conservator;* RPA
8. *The Conservator;* RPA
9. *The Conservator;* RPA
10. *The Conservator;* RPA
11. *The Conservator;* RPA
12. *The Conservator;* RPA
13. Fred Bacon letter; Dale O'Hara Collection
14. The Wm. P. Bull Collection; RPA
15. The Wm. P. Bull Collection; RPA

Chapter 6

Building a Floral Empire

1915 — 1930

Noteworthy Events of the Time

1917 Russian Revolution

1917 Halifax Explosion

1918 End of WW I

1918 - 1919 Influenza Pandemic

1921 Insulin invented

1928 Penicillin invented

1929 Wall Street Stock Market Crash

On August 4, 1914 World War One began when Britain, France and Russia declared war on Germany and the Austro-Hungarian Empire. More than 600,000 men, about 20 percent of the pre-war labour force, were in uniform at a time when the total population of Canada was less than eight million. Seventy-five men from the Dale Estate, many of British ancestry, representing almost 35 percent of its work force, enlisted. Peel County, and Brampton particularly, was heavily involved in the war effort with many farm operations, Dales included, growing extra crops as a patriotic, unselfish service to their brothers overseas. Fields of wheat, potatoes and other root crops were grown to export to the United Kingdom. Both of T.W. Duggan's sons served in the armed forces, as did many other young men from Brampton's early families, such as the Charters, Blains, Bovairds, Harmsworths, Bulls, Prouses and Coopers.

Growth and Economic Prosperity

When the Great War ended on November 11, 1918, it heralded a period of growth and economic prosperity for the town of Brampton. Ground was broken for its very own hospital, spurred by the efforts of the Women's Institutes, local clergy, MPs, doctors, lawyers and businessmen. Brampton became one of the first towns in Ontario to install a municipal sewage treatment plant and by 1920 chlorine was added to the drinking water thus reducing the risk of infection.

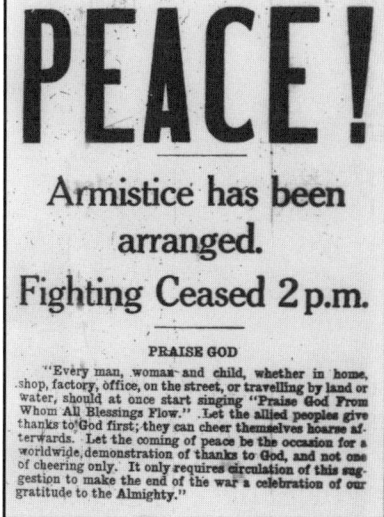

Citizens of Brampton celebrated the end of "the war to end all wars" in November 1918, first in their churches and then in the streets and homes of the town.
Courtesy RPA.

As noted in Loverseed's, *Brampton; an Illustrated History,* *"The population of Brampton by the end of the Great War in 1918 stood at around 4,000. Several companies had moved their operations to Brampton. Firms, involved in a wide variety of enterprises, set up shop — such as Gummed Papers, Brampton Pressed Brick Company, Charters Publishing Company, Copeland Chatterson, Hewetson Shoe Company, which ranked second to Dales during this time period in size, and many others. One of the main reasons such companies were attracted to Brampton was the town's willing and available workforce. Haggert Bros. had failed with the advent of the opening up of the prairies for wheat which was now grown in the west, leaving many local farmers unable to compete and Haggert unable to produce."*

From the same book, researcher Michael Proudlock noted, *"Although many of these industries did not require a large percentage of skilled labour, and those skills which were required could be readily taught, the fact that Brampton possessed a sizable labour pool of men accustomed to working with machinery in the Haggert factory was an added attraction. Labour was very cheap. The workforce was not unionized and teenage boys, some as young as fourteen, were given employment at rock-bottom wages even for that time. Those that had good jobs were lucky to get five cents an hour. The older ones got more but rarely more than ten cents an hour. Most businesses were small with many family-run shops, such as Blain's Hardware and Harmsworth Paint and Wallpaper. It was said of the time that Dales picked up the labour force where Haggert left off."* Within this excellent economic climate, the Dale Estate continued on its upward spiral of success.

The Dale family had grown to adulthood. Ted Dale was listed as a "buyer" for the company, a rather honorific title as Ted never

Ted Dale, his sister-in-law Ann Robinson-Hall, his niece Helen Hall, and Mary French on a summer's outing, c. 1913.
Courtesy Alice Ann Train

participated fully in the business. He and his wife Alice remained in the big Dale home at the southeast corner of Vodden and Main, while Ethel and her husband Bill eventually moved to Main Street North near all of her sisters. The Dales remained dependent upon one another for company with an extremely close bond growing between all of the Dale families. Harry's siblings, Sarah, Will, Ned and Tom also lived close by and all of the immediate and extended families lived near the greenhouses.[1] It was during this time period that the Dales built

The Dale girls and their husbands built summer cottages on the north shore of Lake Bernard, Sundridge, Ontario. (l to r) Rab Campbell, Bud Campbell, Kate Campbell, Jimmy Algie, Sarah Algie, Fan Beatty, Jim Algie, Ethel Dale and Bill Beatty, 1912. Courtesy Judith Vair

Jim Algie, shown with his trumpet, was known for his musical skills and on hot summer nights would serenade the Dale families from his boat on Lake Bernard. (l to r) Sarah Dale and her children Dale, Mary and Jimmy, and Jim, Sr., c. 1915. Courtesy Virginia Gould

Fan Dale Beatty (centre), Ethel Dale Brydon (with pail) and other Beatty women stroll the north shore of Lake Bernard in Sundridge, c. 1914. Courtesy Thomas Brydon Jr.

summer residences on the north shores of Lake Bernard in Sundridge, Ontario, which their descendants continue to occupy to the present day. Algies, Dales, Brydons, Campbells, Halls and Beattys made the annual trek north by train and by motor car to spend the hot summer months in the Almaguin Highlands.

It appeared in 1918 that the Dale family was well on its way to reaping the benefits of Harry's legacy. Someone asked Ted Dale why he let T.W. Duggan earn a sum well into five figures each year from their company. Ted replied, *"It's a lot cheaper for us to hire T.W. Duggan to look after our affairs than it would be for us to try to run the business ourselves."*[2] This rather sums up the way the Dales looked upon T.W. and his business acumen.

Influenza Pandemic

In 1918 the Great Influenza Pandemic hit. It came when the world was weary of war and swept the globe in months, ending when the war did, disappearing as mysteriously as it had appeared. When it was over, humanity had been struck by a disease that killed more people in a few months than any other illness in recent history. Estimates of between 20 million and 100 million people perished worldwide by the time the pandemic had run its course. The sickness preyed on the young and the healthy, namely adults in the 20 to 40 age range. At first, a victim would notice a dull headache, followed by shivers, and then would eventually fall into a restless sleep with nightmares, delirium and high fever. Within a few days or often a few hours, a patient's face would turn a dark brownish purple, they would cough up blood, breathing would become impossible and the victim would die, drowning as their lungs filled with reddish fluid — a truly horrible way to die.

William Beatty, Fan Dale's young husband, came down with the flu. Fan was confined to their house to care for him and, as a precaution, sent her young son William Jr. to her sister Ethel for safekeeping during his father's illness. Elizabeth Brydon Dickson, Ethel's daughter, recalled, *"As a child, I remember my mother taking me and my cousin Billy over to my Aunt Fan's house on Market Street where she was in quarantine. I can still see her in my mind's eye, leaning on the window sill in the upper bedroom window with a scarf tied around her head, talking with my mother as we stood on the sidewalk."* Within days, Fan became infected as well as her brother Ted. The only medicine available to combat the flu was aspirin, which Fan had an aversion to and she would not take any medication. Of Ted, one can only speculate that with his general attitude of devil-may-care, he never thought that he could possibly become infected and would not have taken any precautions. William survived, but both Fan and Ted succumbed to the virus and it rapidly killed them within days of each other; Ted, the son and heir to the family business, died two days before Christmas in 1918 age 33. Fan died at age 31 on December 27. The Dales were devastated by this loss and it was a bleak Christmas for the close-knit family, with Kate Dale Campbell in particular grieving terribly for her twin sister. William Beatty was a widower with a one and half year old to raise on his own, and Alice was now a widow with no prospects of the fame and fortune she expected as Ted Dale's wife. With the passage of

The last known portrait of Ted Dale who died during the Great Flu Pandemic of 1918.
Courtesy Dale O'Hara Collection

time, the remaining family members survived, as did many others in Brampton who had lost loved ones to the epidemic. Kate Dale Campbell and her family moved into the big house on the southeast corner of Main and Vodden, which thereafter became known as the Campbell Residence famed for its circular driveway and spectacular flower beds, lovingly tended by her husband Robert. William Beatty remarried and took a more managerial role in the running of the company and Alice remained a widow, spending her days travelling around the globe and playing aunt to her many nieces and nephews.

The deaths ended the succession from Edward Senior to Harry and to his son Ted, and T.W. Duggan became the defacto successor to Harry Dale. He never owned the business despite several attempts at procuring control, but rather continued to remain as business manager.

T.W. Duggan, managing executor of the Dale Estate, surrounded by flowers ready for the marketplace, c. 1918. Courtesy RPA

The Dale greenhouses covered over 20 acres in which grew roses, carnations, orchids, valley lilies and mums of the highest quality. This view looks westward toward the interesection of Main and Vodden streets, c. 1920.
Courtesy R.L. Frost Collection/ RPA

A Formalized Company

An article in a 1920 edition of *The Conservator* gives a wonderful glimpse into the scope of the business, "*In 1919, there were cultivated 200,000 rose plants, 225,000 carnation plants, 160,000 chrysanthemum plants, 50,000 violet plants, 300,000 bulbs, 60,000 orchid plants, 35,000 asparagus plants, besides sweet peas, ferns, mignonette and gladioli, making a total of one million plants under cultivation. The take of blooms from each of these was in the tens of millions.*

The cold storage plant that cost $10,000 to build contained eight rooms. The walls were lined with insulating slabs of cork and specially designed custom-made doors. In the cold storage area were kept such things as Easter Lily bulbs, which had to be kept at a low temperature before being placed in the warm moist air of the growing houses.

In the 100 foot shipping room, built of reinforced concrete, masses of all sorts of flowers being placed in boxes were readied for shipment, some destined to travel hundreds and thousands of miles. Roses were placed in a cool atmosphere to harden for 24 to 48 hours after cutting before they were shipped. Carnations stayed for 24 hours in the cold. When ready for packing, a wooden box, made on the premises, was lined with from two to six thicknesses of newspaper. Across one end of this was laid a piece of wadding and on the wadding, sheets of waxed paper. The heads of the roses were placed singly in the box and laid on the paper. Each fresh layer of flowers called for more waxed paper. The boxes were never crowded and reached places such as Regina in perfectly good condition. In very hot weather, a small piece of ice was occasionally laid in a box to ensure the necessary moisture. By the position of the handle on the box, express train companies and messengers knew which end of the box contained the heads of the flowers and were handled accordingly.

The huge coal plants and boilers required engineers of the highest quality to keep the houses heated by steam at the required temperature. In 1920, they burned 12,000 tons of coal annually at a cost of $120,000. The great draught chimneys towered over the town. The staff of expert steamfitters constantly engaged in the inspection and repair of pipelines, boiler rooms and radiator pipes, eliminated much of the danger of a freeze up in the cold weather. Foresight with regard to coal purchases and a steam generating plant ensured the continuous supply of heat."

Employees of the Company

The office staff included T.W. Duggan as Managing Executor, J.E. Cooper as Assistant Manager and W.G. Peacock as Accountant. In the shipping room was H.G. Mullis as Head Shipper, T.G. Davis as Assistant Shipper, C.W. Norton as Head Designer and E. Seal as Night Shipper. In the works department were Edward (Ned) Dale as Superintendent and Tom Dale as Assistant Superintendent and Engineer. The Heads of Departments were William Dale (roses) James Young (American Beauty roses) W.G. Perry (valley) W.J. Jones (orchids) A. Elliot (sweet peas) E. Reid, (richmond) W. Mason (carnations) E.A. Parsons (mums) H.C. Newmans (violets) J. Donaldson (bulbs) T. Nixon (steam fitting) D. Sarles (stables) and J. Liske (wire frames), plus 200 employees.

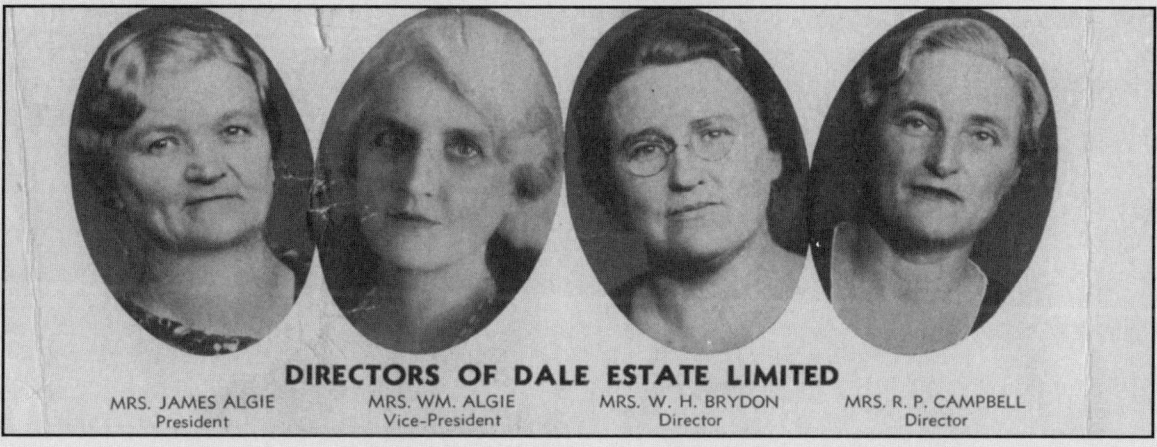

DIRECTORS OF DALE ESTATE LIMITED

MRS. JAMES ALGIE
President

MRS. WM. ALGIE
Vice-President

MRS. W. H. BRYDON
Director

MRS. R. P. CAMPBELL
Director

In 1921 the Dale Estate was incorporated, with the four Dale women, Sarah, Bertha, Ethel and Kate acting as Directors. Courtesy RPA

In 1921, the firm had grown to such a size that it needed to be put on a more solid business foundation and it was duly incorporated as a private limited company. A Board of Directors was created consisting of the remaining four Dale women, Bertha, Sarah, Ethel and Kate. T.W. Duggan was confirmed as the General Manager with dividends given as a share of the profits. He continued to take his salary as part of the yearly profits, a situation that proved to be extremely beneficial, as the company grew increasingly more profitable.

In the years 1900 to 1930, the Dale Estate was extremely successful due largely to the global economic boom times, but credit must also be given to Duggan's astute business practices combined with an extremely talented and dedicated workforce. Dales never experienced a workers' strike over wages at the plant. In an interview with *The Conservator* and *Maclean's* magazine, T.W. gave his reasons for this employee loyalty, the first of which was, "a *revision of the payroll every six months. Every man gets what is fairly and justly coming to him as he has striven during the time. Bonuses are granted in certain departments for productivity and quality control. For instance, American Beauty roses may produce a mass of buds or may develop prickly thickly leafed stalks, eight feet high with never a sign of a bud. Therefore buds mean bonuses."*

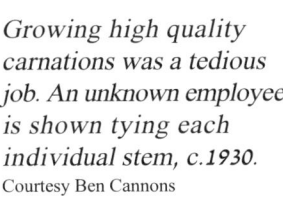

Growing high quality carnations was a tedious job. An unknown employee is shown tying each individual stem, c.1930.
Courtesy Ben Cannons

The second principle Duggan utilized in dealing with his employees was that each man was encouraged to work in his particular department as if the concern belonged to him. "*If he can make useful suggestions, he gets paid for them. The observations and deductions of some worker far away from the heart of the concern may mean an increase in business. He gets a fair share when the payroll is revised."* Third, the employees were encouraged to remain with the firm by being given responsibility. "*Unless an assistant can't handle a situation, I don't want him to come to me. His department is his own concern. If he thinks that my experience may be valuable to him he is welcome to it but it is never thrust upon him. When you pick a man for promotion, it should only be after you have studied him thoroughly and are assured of his ability to handle the job. Don't give a man a job that is too big for him but when you do give it to him, let him run it."*

To Celebrate the Matriarch

Sarah Warren Dale, Harry's mother, was 90 and to celebrate her birthday from the previous December, Bertha Dale Algie, now the proud mistress of the Algie Mansion on the corner of English and

Bertha and William Algie made this lovely mansion their home for many years. Originally owned by the Magill family, who are pictured here, it is situated at the corner of Isabella and English streets and has since been converted to apartments. Courtesy RPA

Isabella streets, threw a party for 60 people on June 16, 1921. Clara Dale Matthews, age 59, Sarah's daughter, had just returned to Canada from her home in Los Angeles, California after an absence of 18 years. In *The Conservator,* it mentioned, *"An entertainment was provided by Sarah's grandchildren and great-grandchildren. Her grandchild, Ethel Dale Brydon, sang while numbers were given by the smaller people, all of whom are musically gifted. A good part of the evening was spent on the lawn and refreshments of ice cream, cake and other good things were served."* Bertha, ever the gracious host but a rather austere, prickly woman, rarely allowed the smaller children into the house and it is doubtful she did even on this occasion. Sarah, who had emigrated with Edward in 1863, the matriarch of the Dale empire, died a few years after this social event at age 93.

Sarah Warren Dale, mother of Harry Dale, on her 90th birthday, December 19, 1920.
Courtesy Dale O'Hara Collection

The CPR station, where Dale flowers were loaded for transportation across Canada and the United States also greeted tourists and travellers to Brampton, c. 1910.
Courtesy R.L. Frost Collection /RPA

New ranges of greenhouses continued to be constructed in the lower flats near the Etobicoke Creek, c. 1930.
Courtesy R.L.Frost Collection/RPA

A Nationwide Business

An early trade publication, *Dale's Book of Floral Supplies*, gives great insight into the business side of the firm. *"We have at last completed and planted a new range 850 ft. x 85 ft. which we consider the finest houses ever built in Canada. This space will be devoted to roses and carnations. September 1 finds all our houses ready and it is with pleasure we can inform our customers of a most promising season's output. With added capacity devoted to the culture of roses, carnations, orchids, valley, lilies, mums and numerous other seasonal flowers, we feel capable of giving you better service than any other firm in America. Our Florists Supplies branch of our business is continually adding new and attractive lines that should be carried by every up-to-date florist. Quality comes first and price second in the proper order of value but we give you both and outdistance all competitors. We employ no travellers and you save by giving us your patronage per mail. Our order department and shipping facilities give you continuous service day and night from 9 p.m. Sunday to 11 p.m. Saturday which means you are in touch with the largest supply in Canada every hour of the business week. Remember you get our stock from us direct in prime condition. We do not ship to commission houses whose extra handling injures the quality. We sell to the trade exclusively. Our transportation facilities are unsurpassed in Canada with 18 trains leaving Brampton starting at 6:52 a.m. through to 11:55 p.m. on the Grand Trunk and Canadian Pacific Railways to all points in Canada and connections to the USA.*[3] The railway system, a vital part of the enterprise, sent all mail directly to the Estate rather than going through the Brampton Post Office. It was sufficient for customers to write "Dales Brampton" on the label, for the company was so widely known that it was considered a post office station on every mail train in Canada.

Dale's nationwide business succeeded due to price, quality, friendship and service. They handled everything that a dealer required, from every kind of flower to baskets, frames designs, paper, twine, ribbons, chiffon, clips, cards and many other items. The result was that most retailers preferred to do all of their business with the company. The personal touch that Harry started was continued by T.W. and he periodically took trips across the continent to renew acquaintances with his customers.

By 1923, the business was valued at $450,000 with 140 acres of land and more than 350 employees. It grew 30 different varieties of flowers, nearly all of which are in the following list in the order of their quantities and importance: roses, carnations, orchids, lilies of the valley, chrysanthemums, sweet peas, violets, Japanese lilies, white and fancy, antirrhinum (snapdragons) marguerites, calendulas, tulips, daffodils, narcissus, paperwhites, narcissus soleil d'or, fresias, gladioli, gypsophilia, peonies, pyrethrum—the daisy family, gaillardia, delphiniums, schillea, scabiosa, statice, celosia and pansies. In what were known as "greetis," they grew asparagus, plumosis, adiantum, maidenhair fern, smilax, mignonette and

The Dale Estate was a tourist feature of the town of Brampton as evidenced in this postcard of the day, c. 1930.
Courtesy R.L. Frost Collection/RPA

fountain grass. In the roses alone, there were 18 different kinds: Angelus, Annie Laurie, American Beauty, Butterfly, Betty Uprichard, Commonwealth, Columbia, Claudius Pernet, Captain Kilbee Stewart, Ethel Somerset, Hoosier, Lady Maureen Stewart, Ophelia, Premier, Rev. Page Roberts, Sunburst, Sweetheart, Premier Sport and seedlings.

In 1924, Dales estimated that they grew more than 12.5 million blooms. Their output was from one-third to one-half of that of all the greenhouses in Canada, adding an estimated one to two million dollars into the economy every year. As a result of their quantity of production, inspection and grading, flowers of varying quality were available to all. Losses were practically unknown. In previous years, tons of lower quality flowers were wasted each year, but now everything was being sold. In a *Maclean's* article, Duggan explained how they managed to keep losses to a minimum. *"We keep here a daily record of sales and production. Each week at least, comparisons are made with the corresponding weeks of former years. In this way we can arrive at a definite forecast of the probable demand. The flowers were graded First, Seconds, Thirds, Fourths, and shorts with the result that retailers are able to make special prices on some of these grades and take our output. Our product is so highly perishable that it was only sound business practice to make this arrangement and to point out to the dealer the advantage of occasional low-priced sales."*[4] For the buying public, a Dale Rose, even of the lower quality, was still a Dale Rose and highly sought after.

Wib Thomson, long time Dale employee, is shown with the morning cut of roses, c. 1947.

Courtesy R.K Cooper Collection/RPA

The Dale Estate exported large amounts of their stock to the United States. In 1925, the USA increased the tariff on cut flowers from Canada, a move directly aimed at the Dale Estate. But even with that, the company could lay down their product, after paying 40 percent duty and transportation charges, at a lower price than similar products could be produced in the States. Dales were able to remain competitive mainly due to the distribution system in operation in the USA, for approximately 95 percent of the florist business in the USA was done through commission houses. Duggan was always ready to eliminate the middleman wherever possible and he therefore sold directly to the retailer. There was one middleman in Canada at this time, the Montreal Floral Exchange that carried stock in a well-kept cold storage area and was able to fill rush orders and take care of emergencies. But throughout most of Ontario, the railway express facilities were so good that Dales could supply the flowers just as quickly as a wholesale distributor.

Other Growers

Many other growers from across the continent would send their sons to work at Dales to "learn the trade." The company generously welcomed these young men, believing that there was room within the industry for everyone, yet knowing that they were of such a size and enjoyed such a high reputation for quality and fairness that they had little to fear from competition. Some of the local people who had learned their trade at Dales went on to found nurseries of their own. One such was the previously mentioned Walter E. Calvert, a hard working man who, after a short six and a half years spent perfecting the growing techniques in a new climate, quit the Dale Estate in 1911 and set up his own business. With true entrepreneurial spirit and hard work, the W.E. Calvert Co. grew to large proportions, specializing in prize-winning chrysanthemums. Likewise Charles Fendley, the nephew of Harry, left Dales in 1919 and re-established his father's nursery business. Jennings Nurseries at the corner of Church and Union streets had been in operation on a small scale since the turn of the century and had developed an expertise in growing carnations. With the increase in the demand for quality flowers, they too were able to expand and consolidate their niche in the floral marketplace. Numerous smaller conservatories opened up across Brampton with most streets in the core of the town sprouting

Walter Calvert
Courtesy *Brampton's 100th Anniversary Book*/RPA

Charles Fendley
Courtesy Charters Collection/RPA

Jennings greenhouses were situated at the corner of Church and Union streets.
Courtesy R.L. Frost Collection/RPA

small greenhouses. Lagerquist, Miller, Gregory and McHardy were but a few of the operations that, although they were not of the size of the Dale Estate, all grew flowers of good quality, earning Brampton the growing reputation as "The Flower Town of Canada."

An Entity Unto Itself

The company at this time had an army of its own workforce from glaziers, welders and carpenters to electricians, steamfitters and plumbers. It had two full time night watchmen and its own small weather station, which was housed inside a wooden box with slats on the sides, located near the "horsewalk" and manned by Wib Thomson. With the advent of the motorcar, trucks replaced the horse-drawn wagons, and mechanics replaced the livery men, although the "horsewalk," where the horses had been stabled, remained a shortcut within the property and retained its name in later years. In the '20s Dales boasted its own mini fire brigade that had its own hose and reel and often supplemented the volunteer Brampton Fire Brigade at town blazes. As well, the company telephone system, with its own internal switchboard, became a more

In June of 1925, a huge hailstorm struck the town of Brampton. This was every florist's nightmare as the greenhouses with their glass construction and precious stock were particularly vulnerable. It was reported that hailstones the size of baseballs hammered the glass of the greenhouses causing tremendous damage. It was estimated that it required 14 railcars of diamond glazed glass to repair the damage to the greenhouses.

Courtesy Darren Spindler Collection

integral part of the business, replacing the importance of the telegraph upon which they had relied so heavily for so long.

The citizens of Brampton had learned to regulate their life by the Dale Estate "clock," which was a steam whistle mounted on the large Dale chimney. When the whistle blew to signal the beginning, middle and end of the working day, it could be heard clear across the town and most townspeople were highly aware of Dale's steady, reliable presence. Men on their bicycles would come streaming to and from the plant, which necessitated the nearby Central Public School to alter their opening and closing times so as not to endanger the children from the rush of bicycle traffic. The greenhouses stretched on both sides of Main Street — on

The Dale Estate employed its own glazier, Bill King, to maintain and repair the over 20 acres of glass.
Courtesy R.K. Cooper Collection/RPA

In 1930, the Dale Estate owned 243 acres of land, of which 35 were under glass. Looking west, the great "Dale Chimney" can be seen in the distance on the right side of the photograph.
Courtesy RPA

the east side, from Rosedale Avenue East north to Vodden Street and east to the Etobicoke Creek and on the west side from Dale and Lorne avenues, north to English Street and west to the CPR railway tracks. It appeared as if the entire north end of the town was a sea of glass, and indeed it was, as the Dale Estate alone had 35 acres under glass.

At the close of 1930, due to its reputation as the premier flower industry of Canada, the Dale Estate figured prominently in the annual Canadian National Exhibition parade of floats. Along the parade route, everyone stared in awe at the multitude of blooms and greenery magnificently displayed in a floral tribute to the third largest greenhouse operation in the world.

Notes

1. Map of Dale Houses/Tunnels/Greenhouses (see Appendix IV);
   Personal Collection, Dale O'Hara
2. *The Conservator*; RPA
3. Jim Taylor Collection
4. *Maclean's* Magazine; Brampton Library Archives

Chapter 7

The Great Depression and the War Years
1930 – 1945

Noteworthy Events of the Time

1930 - 1939 Great Depression

1939 World War II begins

1941 Japan attacks USA at Pearl Harbour

1944 Normandy Invasion

1945 End of World War II

In 1929 the Wall Street Stock Market crash occurred which, coupled with the enormous wheat crop failure of 1928, plunged Canada into what has become known as the Great Depression. The gross national product in Canada fell from $6.1 billion in 1929 to $3.5 billion in 1933 and the value of industrial production halved. The Federal Department of Labour stated that a family needed between $1,200 and $1,500 per year to maintain the minimum standard of living, but during this time 60 percent of men made less than $1,000 annually.

The "Dirty Thirties"

As the Depression carried on into the mid-thirties, commonly known as the "dirty thirties," one in five Canadians became dependent on government relief and 19 percent of the country's labour force was unemployed. Tens of thousands of people across the country were forced to rely on charity and food handouts for daily survival. Parents found it difficult to keep young children in school because they needed them on the farms to bring in as much of their crop as possible. University students from across the country were also dropping out because the cost of tuition, room and board was out of reach. Homemakers had to find part time jobs to "make ends meet." The number of immigrants to Canada dropped significantly and due to illness and unemployment many were forced to go back to their home country.

The federal government enacted many social reform policies, including financial relief programs for families in need. The monthly relief rate for a family of five ranged from between

$17 to $60 per month in various provinces of the country at a time when bread was selling for 10 cents a loaf and butter for 25 cents a pound.

Brampton Fares Well

In comparison to the rest of the country, businesses in Brampton managed to fare quite well during these hard economic times, for the town had a diversified economy with a mix of skilled and unskilled labour. Being close to the city of Toronto, it was still able to tap into that marketplace and yet its distance enabled it to escape the more serious social problems of the big city. The Bell Telephone Company initiated a number of new construction projects during the early 1930s, including the removal of poles and the installation of underground conduits for an extensive telephone cable system. By 1939 the telephone company labour force had doubled. The Peel Memorial Hospital, begun in 1925, embarked on an expansion with an addition started in 1932 bringing the capacity to 36 beds with an additional 10 cots for babies. Hewitson Shoe Company had solidified its market and continued to expand its line even under these adverse conditions.

A number of other businesses, which had begun during the great boom times of 1900 to 1912, continued to hold their heads above water, such as Gummed Papers, Brampton Knitting Mills, Charters Publishing, LePage Soap Products, Aircraft Details, Canada Tampax, Lewis Leather, Imperial Optical, McCulloch Planing Mill, Bray Chick Factory and Canadian Metal Hose. Such was the life of the small town of 5,000 people that no one went without and no one in need of a meal was ever turned away from the back doors of Brampton.

Dales Survives the Depression

The Dale Estate, in particular, as the largest employer in the town demonstrated its care and compassion for its employees during the Depression years. Because of the already low wages and the unskilled nature of the majority of the jobs, there was always room for "one more" on the payroll. In particular, Dales was known throughout the town as a "sports company" with its own basketball, lacrosse and baseball teams. One story related by a former employee was that the baseball team required a pitcher to boost their win column. They found a player of excellent ability, gave him a job requiring little skill, and the company started to win more games! It was also common knowledge that if you sang in the choir of St. Andrew's Presbyterian or Grace United Church you could always get a job at Dales. Although there was a constant changeover in personnel with officially 300 people on staff, in one year of the Depression there were over 1,000 employment records, indicating the ability of the company to add and subtract people in their workforce with relative ease, thus providing much needed income for employees during hard times. Economies were made by initiating a policy that, if there were two adults from the same family working at Dales, one would be let go. Most married women were also laid off, assuming that their husbands had employment elsewhere.

A government regulation also worked in Dale's favour. The company was regarded as a farm, not as a manufacturer. At this time, unskilled immigrants were required to work for one year on a farm in order to achieve landed immigrant status. This proved to be beneficial, as the newcomers were happy to have a job in such desperate times and Dales were happy to be able to pay a very low wage thus cutting their overhead costs. Many only

The Dale Estate had many of their own sports teams that competed in the town's industrial leagues. This lacrosse jersey proudly displayed the Dale name in team competition, c. 1939.
Courtesy RPA

The men and boys who worked in the greenhouses were dedicated to producing high quality blooms. Low wages were balanced by the prestige of being a "Dale's Man," c. 1935.
Courtesy Marilyn Thomson

stayed for the required one year but it did give them a start in Canada.[1] During this time, a typical worker's wage was 25 cents an hour for a fifty-hour week, working daily from eight in the morning until six at night, to bring in a pay package of $12.50 for the week. This was still substantially lower than the average considered by the government of the day as the minimum wage. For top workers, the salary rose as high as 60 cents per hour. In the Depression years, Dales was forced to institute three cuts and for some, the wage was cut in half. Everyone was given a holiday of two weeks but it was without pay and even with these economies, hours of employment had to be cut back. Not one employee however was given notice that their service was no longer required. This enabled the company to reduce the workforce, reduce the payroll and, coupled with other cost control measurements, weather the storm.

Collecting Newspapers for Money

Again as an indicator of their commitment to assist the town and its citizens, Dales initiated the custom of buying used newspapers from local children. The company regularly utilized over 50 tons of newspaper a year in their shipment of flowers. Mostly these "recycled" papers were purchased from the local newspaper companies and then used to line the shipping boxes, thus keeping the flowers cool during shipment. However, every Saturday morning during the Depression, young boys and girls would load up their wagons with collected newsprint from next door neighbours and from houses around the town, roll them into bundles and take them to the shipping room of Dales.

There the newspapers would be carefully weighed on the big shipping room scale and the children would be given one cent per pound for their efforts. It was common knowledge within the firm, and generally ignored, that some adults would bring in rolls of paper as well but would try and weigh their loads down with bricks. It is interesting to note that Dales could have bought newsprint overruns for the same price as they gave to the children but preferred this way as the company could generate extra cash for the local population.[3]

Fred Bacon, a former Dale employee, recalled,

"The whole town seemed to bring its papers, packed on small wagons, big wagons, in small trucks, every kind of conveyance. Some of the wagons got piled pretty high and it wasn't unusual to see a wagon come to grief, and a pile of papers strewn over the road. No trouble with cars in those days, so all the wagons used the road. We would haul our cargo down to the warehouse where they had a big shed. The papers would be weighed and we would receive a slip of paper showing the weight we had brought in. Then we would go up to the office and present the slip to Miss Reynolds and she would pay us for our load. It was quite an operation as the paper had to be either tied in bundles or rolled in rolls."[2]

Children, some as young as 12, were hired during the summer months for 12 cents an hour to weed rose beds in the greenhouses. This was a difficult job but one well-suited to small folk that could crawl under the raised beds. As well, the Dale Estate took on many seasonal workers and provided numerous part time jobs with over 1,000 employed at one point in the mid-thirties and, although no one was getting rich, people were able to earn enough to survive. They were desperate times and the Depression left an indelible mark on those who lived through it.

T.W. Retires

In 1933, the latter years of the Depression, T.W. Duggan retired as General Manager, at age 75. At the time of his retirement, the Dale Estate was Brampton's biggest and most important employer — the largest cut flower industry in the world, with 350 full time employees, over 35 acres of greenhouses and a payroll of $300,000 per year.

In 1933, upon the retirement of T.W. Duggan, William A. Beatty assumed the role of Managing Director of the Dale Estate. He is pictured here standing in the centre amidst employees of the company. Courtesy RPA

At his retirement, T.W. wrote to his staff, *"It is practically impossible for me to speak to, or with, each member of our staff as I would like to do, but I take this opportunity to express to every one of you, from the superintendent down to the youngest apprentice, my deepest gratitude for your hearty co-operation in making this Dale Estate Limited the largest and finest organization of its kind in the world. I do not claim credit other than being leader of a lot of loyal men and women who have been true to me, and hand-in-hand, have worked together loyally and well to achieve this end and on retiring from the managerial chair, I wish to offer you a loudest and deepest thank you."*[4]

By all accounts from both news articles of the time and from personal recollections and interviews with former employees, T.W. Duggan was a "good man" and a "good manager." Duggan remained on as advisor and counselor and, no doubt weighed down by his advancing years and the effects of the global Depression, he died five years later in 1938.

The New Regime

As before, the managerial succession was in place and the expertise in floriculture was still firmly in the hands of Harry's brothers, Tom, Will and Ned, as well as other old time employees. William Beatty, the widowed husband of Harry's daughter Fan, had joined the firm in 1918. Born and raised in Brampton, William, or W.A. as he was known, had worked in the wilds of northern Ontario from 1912 to

In 1935, most of the 400 employees of the Dale Estate gathered for a company photograph in front of the boiler room located on the west side of Main Street. Courtesy Dale O'Hara Collection

1918 as a prospector for a mining company. It was said that he had slept one night on the biggest gold mine that was discovered in the north in later years, and unknowingly, had failed to stake it! After Fan's death in 1918, W.A. sat on the Board of Directors in Fan's place and in 1921, he was appointed Secretary-Treasurer, a position he held until being appointed the Managing Director upon Duggan's retirement.

The other members of the Board of Directors were the Dale women, with Sarah Dale Algie as President, Bertha Dale Algie as Vice-President, and Kate Dale Campbell and Ethel Dale Brydon as Directors. In control of the plant were Harry's brothers, Edward (Ned) Dale as General Superintendent, William Dale as Assistant Superintendent and Thomas Dale as Construction Superintendent. William's son, Perce Dale, was the Heating Engineer. More family members were employed in the managerial side as the business continued to expand. Bertha's son, Malcolm Algie, was added to the office staff in accounts, and another son, Harry Algie, in the sales force. Sarah's son, James Algie went into accounts and Ethel's son-in-law, Douglas Dickson into the sales force. Not all the family worked in the firm, but certainly enough did that it could still be considered a "family-run" business.

The Dale Autographed Rose

In 1934, Harry Algie came up with a unique marketing plan. *"After four years of patient and intensified research, Dale Estate Limited has been fortunate in discovering a perfect method of identification, the autographing of a rose leaf with DALE."*[5] Perhaps with the change in management and with a younger man at the helm, this scheme bore fruit and the "Autographed Rose" came into being. During the grading procedure for the roses, which consisted of sorting the size of the bloom and the length of the stem into various qualities, one leaf of the highest graded rose was perforated with the name "DALE" by an ingenious punching machine.

Several women had the job of working the stamping machines that autographed the roses, (l to r) Dorothy McVean, Ethel Donnelly, Merle Cardinal and Helen (Smith) Cooper, c. 1947. Courtesy R.K.Cooper Collection/RPA

"The Dale Autographed Rose." In 1934 the Dale Estate became famous for perforating their name on one leaf of their highest quality rose.
Courtesy Jim Taylor Collection

Young Harry had inherited his grandfather's inventiveness and ingenuity and the autographed rose was born.

This gimmick, for that was what it was, was patented and quickly became the signature for the company as demand for the very best, the "Dale Autographed Rose," spread across the marketplace. The autographed roses won prizes at flower shows in Detroit and New York and were shipped to every corner of the globe. Fresh Dale Autographed Roses were sold in the capitals of France and England and became the symbol for perfect quality, matchless colour and lingering fragrance. By providing a permanent protected identification, the autographed rose became the greatest achievement in the merchandizing of cut flowers. In an interview with a woman from the era, she stated, *"When you received a box of Dale Autographed Roses, you knew they were something very special. They came in their own box with the Dale name on the side, beautifully arranged so that the blooms were carefully displayed, with no heads touching each other and all carefully folded in green tissue paper. The stems were perfectly straight and well formed with not a thorn to be seen and then you'd see the Dale name on one of the leaves — just beautiful!"*

Volumes of Blooms Continue to Grow

By 1935, the Depression had started to lift and once again the economy began to pick up, beginning the second wave of unprecedented growth in the company. Under the direction of the new management the business continued to produce crops of the finest quality. Although the worst years of the Depression were over, the big economic "boom" years of the early 1900s and 1920s were not to be repeated. The expansion of the greenhouses slowed but production, measured in the number of blooms cut per year, maintained the volume first recorded in 1923 at 12.5 million annually. Over 30 different varieties of flowers were grown and new varieties of roses were continually being developed. Three varieties of pink roses — Canadian Queen, Lady Canada and Lady Willingdon — were highly praised within the industry. The newly developed roses — Dorothy Dale, Sunbeam and Rosedale — carried the highest awards at the various trade shows across the continent, one of which was the Blue Ribbon in the New York Flower Show for First Ranking Display of Roses in Show.

Rose growing had become a fine art at the Dale Estate requiring dedicated employees and supervisors to ensure their high productivity and quality. For example, in order to achieve the high quality of the long stemmed Autographed Rose, the growers had to pinch off the first buds to form, thus producing longer and stronger stems with finer and hardier blooms. This was a task that could only be done one rose bush at a time, one stem at a time. The actual growing of the roses required constant renewal of the soil, weeding of the rose beds by hand and finally tying up the prickly roses — tasks often performed by high school students. *"As kids, we were tying up the roses one day when Ned Dale came through the door. He walked down to where we were working and he was not amused. All the way down the bed there were pieces of string about an inch long. One of the lads was not tying properly. Ned said, "You never, ever, cut both ends of the string. You only cut one end. You make the tie, and leave only enough string so that you cut one end only. Do you realise how much string you are wasting when you cut both ends?"*[6]

Dales produced millions of blooms yearly, all harvested by a team of dedicated workers such as Tommy Thomson, c. 1940. Courtesy Marilyn Thomson

The Great Depression and the War Years　83

> *Roses represented approximately 65 percent of Dale's total volume of flowers. In 1935 their published statistics were as follows:*
>
> *4,500,000 roses*
> *1,500,000 carnations*
> *1,000,000 lily of the valley*
> *1,500,000 bulbs*
> *700,000 chrysanthemums*
> *250,000 orchids*
> *200,000 lilies*
> *100,000 hot house tomatoes*
> *10,000 English cucumbers*
>
> *Plus thousands of other varieties of flowers, flowering plants, foliage and decorative plants.[7]*

All of the flowers were distributed solely through the Florists of Canada with no retail business being entered into. The Florist Supply end of the company became more important at this time, with florists the length and breadth of the country purchasing not only their flowers but also all of their supplies from the Dale Estate. The orchid trade alone was extremely popular and profitable with over 500 different varieties being grown.

The Dale Chimney – A Brampton Landmark

The greenhouses continued to be heated by steam pipes, with massive boilers kept in pristine working order by steamfitters and stationary engineers. The steam pipes were said to exceed over 100 miles, and one was a continuous welded pipe, eight inches in diameter and over 1,000 feet in length.

The relatively new boiler room was built around 1929 with six main furnaces in continuous operation that were capable of producing 6,000 BTU for each boiler. The building itself was approximately 40 feet high taking approximately 16,000 to 19,000 tons of coal annually to stoke the boilers. During one particularly severe cold weather time, almost ten tons of coal were used in just one hour.[8] For ease of delivery of the coal required by the furnaces, the Canadian Pacific Railway had constructed a spur line that left the main track and ended at the side of the boiler room. A 300-foot chimney was constructed for this heating plant and could be seen across the town of Brampton, becoming a noted landmark. The large bold "DALES"

The massive coal-fired burners required constant stoking, utilizing up to 19,000 tons of coal each year, c. 1935.
Courtesy RPA

in white letters down its side was clearly visible for miles around and became a local landmark for aircraft landing at Malton Airport. The first chimney that was built blew down in a wind storm such was its height but it was quickly rebuilt with a unique brick design that proved to be extremely stable. Each brick was tapered toward the centre line of the chimney and had a curved, glazed outer facing. The bricks became smaller towards the top, but each had a series of square holes running through it from top to bottom, making it resemble a honeycomb. The mortar between the bricks was forced into the holes to give it a grip like masonry fingers.

The Dale chimney, built around 1929, was a Brampton landmark towering 300 feet above the ground. Courtesy Iris Tuckey

The Great Depression and the War Years   85

Counter-clockwise, the houses of Sarah Algie, Ethel Brydon, Thomas Dale, Ned Dale and Will Dale, most of which were heated by steam from the greenhouses. All of these houses are in existence today but without the steam heat connection, c. 2002.
Courtesy Dale O'Hara Collection

It is interesting to note that most of the Dale family homes and some of the houses the family owned that were rented to employees were connected into the steam heating system. The Dale homes which were heated in this manner were at 249 (Ethel Dale Brydon) and 250 Main Street North (Thomas Dale), 36 Lorne Street (Sarah Dale Algie), both Dale homes on the northeast and southeast corners of Vodden and Main, and Bertha Dale Algie's home at 7 English Street. Most of the homes on the southeast side of Rosedale Avenue East were family-owned workers' cottages and were also heated by steam, bringing the total of steam-heated houses to 15.

As mentioned previously, a steam whistle mounted on the side of the great chimney signalled the start of each working period. It also served as a direction indicator for the local volunteer firemen. Each firebox or street alarm box located around Brampton had its own call number that the Dale whistle interpreted as a series of long and short blasts. For example, a long blast equalled ten and a short blast equalled one, which meant Box 32 would be three longs and two short blasts. This was extremely reliable for the town as someone was always on duty in the building due to the nature of the florist business and, of course, because of its height, the whistle could be heard all across the town of 5,700 people. In the event of a fire, a person would run to their local firebox and pull the alarm, which would in turn ring at Dales and the fire station. Dales would then give the location through the whistle signal, and the volunteer firemen would spring into action. Most of the townspeople knew the number of their local firebox and the others across the town, and would know more or less where the fire was located because of the signal from the Dale whistle.

The Tunnel System

By this time greenhouses were built up on both sides of the main street of Brampton, so in order to facilitate the transportation of the steam pipes from one side of the main road to the other, long tunnels had been built. The largest of these connected the west to the east side of the street, running from the main boiler room at the corner of Dale Avenue and Main Street to the greenhouses on the opposite side. Most of the tunnels were six to eight feet wide and seven to eight feet in height, built with concrete walls and a centre walkway. The tunnels were not only used as steam pipe conduits but also for the transportation of labourers and material, particularly in the winter months. This enabled the delicate blooms to remain within a heated environment on their way to the shipping room. Many smaller tunnels connected and branched from this main tunnel and it was estimated at the time that if connected end to end the tunnels would add up to over one mile.

Generations of children, both within the family and without, would use the tunnels as playgrounds and as a way of moving through the town on cold winter days to get to school. Bert Post wrote a wonderful account of such an adventure whereby he and friends would enter the greenhouses at the extreme north end and then race through the greenhouses and the tunnels emerging near the playground of Central Public School. As Bert recollected it was always a challenge to see how far they could get before they were caught by the workers and asked to leave.[9] Ben Cannons had similar memories of he and his friends, who as teenagers worked in the greenhouses during the summer months, wolfing down their lunches in order to have "play time" in the tunnels before they had to return to work. The light switches were at either end of the main tunnel, which was long enough that you could not see the end as it sloped downwards under the street. The main object of the pranks and games of the children was to catch someone unexpectedly in the middle of the tunnel, race towards one end and turn the lights out, leaving the person alone in the pitch dark with just the hissing of the steam pipes to fuel the imagination. Few children grew up in Brampton during those times that had not experienced the perceived terror of the Dale tunnels.

The immensity of the greenhouses was overwhelming. If stood end to end they stretched 9 miles with over 32 miles of walkways. Covering a total of 35 acres in glass, the 132 greenhouses were often used as a playground for the Dale children. Elizabeth Brydon Dickson, Harry's granddaughter, recounted childhood memories of the Dale Estate. *"Every Saturday we would play in the greenhouses, even taking a lunch over. My mother would always warn us about bothering the men in the greenhouses, and to be careful around the flowers. We would*

This view looking northwest shows the vast acreage of Dale greenhouses on both sides of Main Street and the Dale chimney in the distance, c. 1948. Courtesy RPA

help the men in the shipping room, packing the flower boxes with ice, riding the elevator which was a large flat platform that was hauled up and down from the cellar to the shipping room by way of counterweights or a pulley system. The men in the cellar all wore heavy clothing because of the low temperatures. At Easter particularly the cellar would just be a sea of roses. There was also an intercom system to the cellar so that when they called down an order, the order was put on the elevator and then you hauled on the rope to raise the platform to the shipping area. We used to run all over the greenhouses. We never touched any of the flowers but we would pick up any broken ones on the floors. We also used to play where they built the boxes. Originally they were made out of wood and were piled sky high. There was a slide down to the shipping department and when a box was needed, it was just pushed down the slide. We used to push them around to make little houses for ourselves to play in. Down in the flats, the greenhouses were constructed a little differently. The aisles were raised and the rose beds were lower. When we played there we had to jump the beds. I remember mostly the smell of the flowers and the constant hiss of the steam pipes."[10]

Most of the jobs in the greenhouses required individual hand work such as tying up the stalks of the sweetpeas. Shown here with the day's harvest is Caroline (Eddy) Jarvie, c. 1947. Courtesy R.K. Cooper Collection/RPA

This same scenario was played out by future generations as Harry's great grandchildren played in the greenhouses and in the tunnels. The workers were extremely tolerant of the owners' children!

Special Flowers for Special Occasions

One of biggest challenges for the Dale Estate at this time was to force the blooms to coincide with Mother's Day, Valentine's Day, Easter and Christmas. Each holiday had its particular flower that was in high demand. For example for Valentine's Day it was red roses, forget-me-nots and violets and for Christmas it was again red roses. A typical order for a florist such as a Montreal retailer would be 40,000 roses for Mother's Day. Flowers became popular not only for funerals and weddings but as a decorating trend. In 1938 white was fashionable and hence the production and sale of lily of the valley were greatly affected. For corsages white gardenias were the flowers of choice. These were particularly difficult to force and needed to be grown in greenhouses at very high temperatures with only one in four buds actually making it to market. The white orchids were the rarest of those grown and the most expensive. The selling price at this time was $2 and up for one bloom, with one particular orchid plant valued at over $300. Orchids could not be forced into bloom and were therefore highly prized by the consumer and a profitable product for most florists. On one occasion alone, 10,000 orchids were shipped to a major United States retailer.

Tailoring the delicate gardenias into corsages was a highly-skilled job for young women. Pictured is Peggy Burns on the right with an unknown co-worker, c. 1947. Courtesy R.K. Cooper Collection/RPA

Special Shipping Care

To ship the blooms to market in such pristine condition was an art form that the Dale Estate had perfected over the years. The successful storage of their roses and other blooms ensured that the flowers remained in the desired state of maturity, that is, the tightness of the flower buds, as well as retaining their original colour. Dales used

---

Florence Mowat, a former Dale employee, recalled that:

"At Christmas, Easter and Mother's Day, plants were grown especially for these special times. The plants would be blooming row after row. They were so beautiful and a trip across the road from the office to the plant department was a must at these special times of the year for most of the employees." [11]

low temperatures in their storage area, referred to as "the cellar," with proper relative humidity, as well as monitoring the optimum amount of time they were held in storage before shipping. Great care was given to the amount of carbon dioxide present, ensuring no petal drop, loss of colour or opening of the buds. They also had the right mixture of water, sucrose and a salt of certain heavy metals for their containers thus maintaining cut roses and blooms of the highest quality. For protection during shipping, the flowers were placed in wooden boxes for distant markets, and corrugated cardboard boxes for local markets, all assembled on site. The boxes were then lined with layers of newsprint, crushed ice from Dale's own ice making machine and topped with wet newsprint. Their refrigeration plant was capable of making over 20 tons of ice in a year. The orchids were shipped with their stems encased in little glass tubes.

Flowers were kept in the refrigerated cellar until shipment ensuring their freshness and high quality, c. 1950.
Courtesy R.K.Cooper Collection/RPA

Shown here is Tony Stapleton carefully individually packing the flowers for shipping across the continent. The Dale Estate used over fifty tons of newsprint yearly for this task, c.1947.
Courtesy R.K. Cooper Collection/RPA

The Great Depression and the War Years   91

The Dale Design Department created a stunning bridal bouquet of red roses for Harry Dale's granddaughter, Elizabeth Brydon for her wedding on September 18, 1935.
Courtesy Dale O'Hara Collection

Florence Mowat recalled, *"The main building of the Dale Estate was located on Rosedale Avenue on the east side of Main Street North. It was a very large building, which housed the executive offices and general offices on the ground floor and upstairs levels. A connecting door led into the shipping room where the cut fresh flowers and greenery were packed. On both sides of the shipping area there were approximately eight stations where the packers did their work. Adjoining the shipping area was the Order Office and switchboard and the Invoicing Department. Also located off the Shipping Room was the Design Room where the beautiful floral designs were created by three or at times four special designers for weddings, funerals or other requests. On the lower level of the Shipping Room was a vast refrigerated area known as the Cellar. Each day the fresh cut flowers from the various greenhouses were taken into the Cellar where they were put into containers of cold water waiting for the day's orders to be filled.*

They would then be put on the elevator to go up to the shipping area for packing. Early mornings were extremely busy getting the delivery trucks packed and ready to take off for the out-of-town deliveries and for the trains. There was a pneumatic tube system in operation between the Order Department, Supply Department, Invoicing and Shipping Room. It was used every day and expedited orders and invoices to the various departments. The order was rolled up and put into a leather tube and put into the pipe where in seconds it would reach its destination and the order would be filled."[12]

Walter Edwards delivered as well as collected payment for flowers shipped on the Toronto-Hamilton truck route, c.1940
Courtesy Ruth Edwards

The War Years

At the end of the 1930s the business was stable and prosperous despite the aftermath of the Great Depression and looming talk of another war. In 1938, Kate Dale Campbell died and shortly thereafter, war was declared on Germany. Throughout the years of 1939 to 1945, Brampton and the Dale Estate sent many of its finest young men to war. Many of the younger workers in the firm enlisted and family members, such as Stuart Beatty brother of W.A. Beatty, Douglas Dickson, son-in-law to Ethel Dale Brydon, and young Edward Dale Brydon, joined up and were either shipped overseas or involved in the war effort away from Brampton. For those men who were of retirement age, their loyalty to the firm was needed and most of them, if they were able, stayed on to help out the family. Youngsters, too young to enlist, were hired on a part time basis and yet again, the Dale Estate managed to keep its business afloat through the difficult years from 1938 to 1945.

Brampton's own Lorne Scots fought in almost every theatre that involved Canadian troops. The local paper, *The Conservator*, kept the town informed, bringing daily war news from the battlefields as well as reporting on activities at home with its pages filled with numerous fundraising campaigns organized by various church groups, social clubs and charities. Young pilots in training often used the sun glinting off the Dale greenhouses to guide them to a safe landing in Malton as well as the big Dale chimney as a landmark for navigation. Many of the young men of Brampton did not

Parades to celebrate the end of WWII and numerous receptions honouring those who had served in the war were held in churches, theatres, and parks across the town, c. 1945. Courtesy RPA

return; 58 were killed, one of them was Ted Dale Brydon, Harry Dale's grandson. His mother Ethel Dale Brydon had died suddenly in the spring of 1943, as well as his aunt, Bertha Dale Algie in 1944. Both Tom and Will Dale, Harry's brothers, died in 1940 and 1944 respectively. Only Ned, the sole surviving brother, and Sarah Dale Algie, Harry's sole surviving child, were left of that generation to carry on the Dale name.

The end of World War II, on August 14, 1945 brought huge celebrations throughout the country and the small town of Brampton. *"The crowd unprecedented in Brampton history packed Gage Park yesterday afternoon to attend the Thanksgiving Peace Service. Prior to the service a parade formed at Rosalea Park and paraded down Main Street to music of the Lorne Scots Pipe Band, Salvation Army Band, and the Brampton Brass Band."*[13]

The Flower Town of Canada Continues to Prosper

Despite the horrors and the chaos in Europe, the war years did boost the economy with Canada becoming one of the major arsenals and supply base for Britain. The Dale Estate continued to be the greatest single employer and most important capital-producing business in Brampton. To man this huge enterprise were 400 employees, the majority working a 50-hour week in the lush, mostly humid and overpoweringly fragrant workplace. Along with other major industries such as the Hewetson Shoe Company, Brampton enjoyed moderate success as a town isolated from the greater social impact of war, in part due to the generally slower communication systems of rail, air, road, telephone and telegraph. Its agricultural heritage was prosperous and a sense of well-being infused every part of the town's character. Spired, turreted, and well-attended Protestant churches abounded. There was an active ballpark and bandstand, and a wooden building containing a curling rink which catered to both the young and the old. The annual Fall Fair linked the town and the surrounding rural area, and a fine courthouse and imposing Edwardian and Victorian mansions in park settings lined the main street. Brampton boasted low taxes, clean air, better than average schools including a high school, with two-thirds of all houses being owner-occupied and almost entirely single-family dwellings.

Many young boys started their working career at Dales during the depression and war years. Here one such employee proudly displays an armful of the day's cut of sweetpeas, c. 1940. Courtesy Marilyn Thomson

Located on Main Street North, Grace United Church was built in 1867 and enlarged in 1888. This early photo of the 1890s shows the magnificent brickwork and soaring spire common in churches of this period. Courtesy /RPA

"The Flower Town of Canada" enjoyed a largely middle class existence, whose demographics had not dramatically changed since its founding, whose businesses thrived and whose citizens counted themselves fortunate to live in Brampton.

Notes

1. Interview with Douglas Dickson by Finn O'Hara 1990; RPA
2. Fred Bacon letter; Dale O'Hara Collection
3. Interview with Jim Algie 1990 by Finn O'Hara; RPA
4. Brenda Duggan Charters Collection
5. The Wm. P. Bull Collection; RPA
6. Fred Bacon letter; Dale O'Hara Collection
7. The Wm. P. Bull Collection; RPA
8. The Wm. P. Bull Collection; RPA
9. RPA
10. Interview Elizabeth Brydon Dickson
11. Interview Florence Mowat
12. Interview Florence Mowat
13. *The Conservator*; RPA

Chapter 8

Brampton Boom Times
1945 — 1955

Noteworthy Events of the Time

1949 Newfoundland joins Confederation

1950 - 1953 Korean War

1953 Stratford Festival begins

1954 First subway opens in Toronto

1954 Hurricane Hazel rips through Southern Ontario

A t the end of the war Canada, and Brampton in particular, was set to experience the greatest demographic shift of the century. Not since the boom years of 1900 to 1912, with its increase in population and immigration, had Brampton experienced such unprecedented growth. The men returned from the war and the population explosion was on. The birth rate went up dramatically and new immigrants from the war-torn countries of Europe made their way to Canada. Many of those new Canadians had come from The Netherlands and naturally felt right at home in the flower industry. In 1943, the population of Brampton was 6,020. Five years later it had grown by 750, and within ten years, in 1953, the population was 10,366, a rise of 4,346 persons or a 42 percent increase.

The "Baby Boom" Era

In 1945, scattered across Brampton were approximately 200 separate greenhouses ranging anywhere in length from 850 feet to just 40 feet. The largest ones belonged to the Dale Estate, followed by those of Calvert, McHardy, Lagerquist, Neudoeffer, Plested, Tranby, Jennings, Gregory, Miller and a host of smaller one and two-greenhouse operations. With the rise in population or 'baby boom', which was seen right across the continent, came a rapidly-growing economy and expansion once again at the Dale Estate. Most of the men returning

Looking east toward the intersection of Main and Vodden streets, the 132 Dale greenhouses housed over one million cultivated plants, c. 1950. Courtesy Philip Gauthier; photograph by Tom Brydon

from the war went back to their former employment and the majority of the young men and women hired during the war stayed on. One such person, Glynne Everson, recalled, *"I started working for Dales in 1940. They put out a call to the principal of the high school for an "office boy" to replace Alan Hore who had joined the air force. I could type and was in the commerce course and so I was hired. I had a really interesting job because not only did I do the accounts receivable, I got to sit at the front office and greet customers and visitors and show people around the place, which happened almost daily."*

Rose Days

It was reported that in 1949 the Dale Estate cut and shipped 5.75 million roses alone and in this same year the Town, in conjunction with Dales, the Rotary Club and local businesses instituted "Rose Days." Beautiful bunches of Dale roses were sold in various local shops across Brampton in aid of charity. It was a wonderful opportunity for locals to purchase single roses at a good price as Dales was strictly a wholesale operation and normally did not sell directly to the public. Wally Large, a Brampton druggist, is pictured with a young lady selling Dale roses for charity, c. 1949.

Courtesy R.K. Cooper Collection/RPA

By 1948, Dales had increased to a total of 132 greenhouses. Production remained steady at ten million blooms cut per year with over one million cultivated plants. In an article in *The Toronto Telegram*, Dales was described as, *"Peculiarly Canadian, the Dale Estate executives are not greatly impressed with the magnitude of their enterprise. You could pass the place quite easily going north out of Brampton, so small and inconspicuous is the signboard marking the main office. But you cannot escape seeing the giant chimneys and vast expanse of glass on either side of the highway. Visitors are welcomed at the place and veterans steeped in the lore of their specialty and, whether it be the glamorous orchid, the infinite variety of roses, or the operation of grafting, are glad to enlighten the visitor."*[1]

In the years after the war ended, the company converted from coal to oil. For years those people living in the shadow of the great Dale chimney had put up with the falling coal dust, particularly on wash days. One person recalled, *"The women used to hang out their washing knowing that they would have to give it all a good shake before they brought it inside to get the coal dust off. It would just settle on anything that was hung out to dry. I'll tell you they were pretty happy when Dales finally got rid of those old burners!"*[2]

In 1947 the coal-fired furnaces were replaced by oil boilers. Shown here is Percy Cox, the chief engineer, checking on Valve #2 boiler, c. 1947. Courtesy R.K. Cooper Collection/RPA

Switching to oil was seen at the time to be a cheaper, cleaner fuel and more efficient method of doing business. Instead of the old coal burning giants, seven boilers were installed, burning 15,000 gallons of oil daily, or approximately 3 million gallons per year, with a capacity of 7,000 HP. This new system supplied the steam heat to all of the greenhouses, buildings and family homes. The chief engineer Percy Cox constantly maintained not only the boilers but also the auxiliary coal burning plant, which was kept operational for emergencies.

Loyal Employees

The Dale Estate of this time period was an efficient company, with an amazing array of professionals on staff. In addition to their substantial office force of accountants, managers, sales staff, secretarial staff, shippers and general workers, several of their 400 employees were listed as professional growers, such as Arthur Clifford and Charlie Hotchkiss.

A conference of the Dale Estate executives, c. 1947 (l to r): John Beatty, D'Arcy Duggan, W.A. Beatty, Doug Dickson and Tommy Davis.
Courtesy R.K.Cooper Collection/RPA

It was also at this time that the business came to the attention of the unions. It was well known that the company paid low wages and few benefits for long hours, an ideal climate for a union takeover. The United Mine Workers Union, who represented any industry deriving their existence from working with soil, made a bid to unionize the Dale Estate workers, but failed in their attempt. Most of the employees were quite satisfied with their jobs and the family atmosphere of the company. Perhaps as a result of this threat of unionization, the company began various initiatives to ensure the loyalty and satisfaction of their employees, such as elected representatives to management and matching canteen profits to benefit the workers.

Most of the older generation that had been with the company for 50 years finally were able to retire in 1952. Harry's brother Ned left the firm he had helped nurture

Ned Dale, pictured on the left, and Tommy Davis worked side by side for over 50 years at the Dale Estate, c.1947. Courtesy R.K. Cooper Collection/RPA

and grow since its inception. Dubbed "Harry's Good Men," Tommy Davis, the shipping supervisor, Wib Thomson, Tommy Nixon, Billy Little and Tommy Lockhurst, to name but a few, were honoured for their many years of service to the firm. In mid-1952, when the company formed their Twenty-five Year Club, 69 men and women qualified as inaugural members, having 25 plus years of service with the company. Five of the men had been with Dales for over 50 years with another eight having served for periods ranging between 40 and 50 years. In her message to the new club members, Sarah Dale Algie was quoted as saying, *"I welcome the opportunity to say a few words to you. They are words of appreciation for the years of service given to the Dale Estate by the 69 men and women who are charter members. It is the kind of faithfulness and loyalty to the firm which you have exhibited over these many years that has enabled the Dale Estate to keep on providing jobs year after year for about 350 men and women."*[3]

The Twenty-Five Year Club

The names honoured at the inaugural meeting of Dale's Twenty-five Year Club as reported in the May 10, 1952 issue of Canadian Florist Magazine, *are like a "Who's Who" of early Brampton:*
First row (l to r) H. Boothroyd, F. Wilcox, E. Switzer, H. Algie, H. Bailey, C. Bacon, D. Duggan, J. Wood, J. Lamb, W. Haines, W. Windridge, H. Winter, C. Bailey, H. Cuthbert, T. Tullett, P. Cox.
Second row (l to r) J. Burrell, S. Dale-Algie, E. Gregory, A. Clifford, R. Edy, C. Nixon, W. Little, J. Ackroyd, J. McDonald, W. Thomson, B. Keegan, W. Buchanan, F. Merritt, G. Potter, W. Nicholls, C.Green.
Third row (l to r) W. A. Beatty, J. Cresswell, R. Nyberg, A. Jeans, J. Mair, H. Harvey, C. Hotchkiss, H. Morris, L. Davey, W. Morris, F. Bacon, R. Ingram, A. Hamilton, R. Tait, G. Moore, F. Wilson, A. McCarroll,
Back row (l to r) A. Masternak, E. Dale, T. Nixon, H. Teasdale, J. Donaldson, J. Savage, C. Gordon, B. Cook, W. Goddard, W. Cuthbert, W. Waller, H. Davenport, Wib Thomson, T. Davis, J. Morris, W. Aitchison, S. Goodhew.

Courtesy RPA

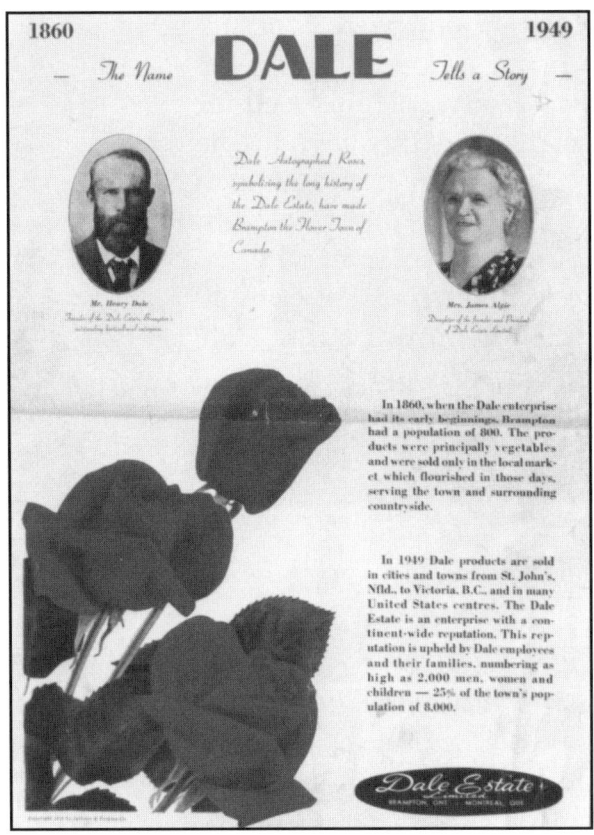

A *1949* advertisement extols the virtues of the Dale Autographed Rose. Courtesy Dale O'Hara Collection

Sarah Dale Algie, the sole surviving child of Harry Dale, was to remain involved with the company until her retirement in 1957. She took an active role in the directorship of the company, serving as president, then in her later years as chairman of the board. *"During those years of wartime expansion, Depression and a second war, I missed very few meetings of the board. There was scarcely a week went by that I did not walk over to the plant to see how the crops were doing and to talk with the men. It's in my blood I guess. I have always loved flowers; I still like to go out into my garden or over into the greenhouses, and I like people. I think of the many men who have worked for us and then gone out on their own. Little did my father and I think, in those early days, that one day the business that was so small would have a host of other businesses start from it. We have seen our own business grow to unique proportions, and also, throughout the West, in BC and even right here in Ontario, there are many businesses whose founders were trained at Dales. It is nice to feel that you have been a part of something that is good and beautiful and useful."*[4]

Dale's Flowers Enjoyed by Royalty

TCA stewardesses hold the bouquets of Dale roses destined for Princess Elizabeth, c. 1951.
Courtesy Dale O'Hara Collection

In 1951 Dales was chosen to send 50 autographed premium red roses to Princess Elizabeth, as she was then, to be presented to her on her tour of Canada. They were first flown to England and then accompanied Her Highness on her flight to Canada and another bouquet was presented to the

Carol Smith from Lakeview is dwarfed by the long-stemmed roses which were to be presented to the Royals, 1951. Courtesy Charters Collection/RPA

Upon her arrival at Malton Airport in October 1951, Princess Elizabeth was presented with a bouquet of Dale Autographed Roses. Courtesy Charters Collection/RPA

Princess upon her arrival at Malton Airport. In the following year, for her 1952 coronation as Queen Elizabeth II, a bouquet of yellow roses named Queen Elizabeth, in honour of the Queen Mother, whose stems measured three feet in length, were shipped to Buckingham Palace for the grand occasion. In the same year, the Right Honourable Vincent Massey, Governor General of Canada, made a trip to tour the greenhouses and extended his planned 20 minute tour to over two hours, such was his "fascination with the extensive growing operation."

Soil Cultivation and Rose Grafting

The company owned 250 additional acres of farm-land to the west of the town near McLaughlin Road, which were used for soil cultivation and crops. It was an essential part of the flower industry that proper soil and fertilizer be used in order to grow the best quality blooms. Since the

Assisted by Ethel Markell, Harry Dale Jr. regularly conducted soil tests to ensure the proper growing medium for all flowers, c. 1950. Courtesy R.K. Cooper Collection/RPA

early years this task had been performed by "The Gang". Enriched, composted soil and cow manure were brought in from the farm, and the gang would shovel the old soil from the beds and dispose of it. The new soil would be sterilized with steam from the boilers and the rose plants changed.[5] Pipes carrying the fertilizer to the greenhouses totalled two and a half miles in length. Meticulous records were kept of the laboratory soil tests for nutrients and acidity, both ingredients crucial to rose growing. These tests were carried out on an ongoing basis by Harry Dale Jr., grandson of William Dale. The rose houses were undoubtedly the focus of the operation, with most measuring 863 feet in length and containing approximately 50,000 plants. Such care was taken in their cultivation that it is no wonder they were of the very highest quality. In the early years, employees painstakingly syringed each plant to keep the bushes free of aphids. With newer chemicals discovered during the war, the task of syringing became minimal, and regular hand spraying with pesticides became the preferred method for pest control.

The cutting was usually done in the early morning while the roses were in bud. In order to produce the quality and quantity needed, renewing their rose stock was a constant job which was done by their highly trained workforce. Grafting of the rose scion onto a Manetti rootstock was a delicate, highly skilled operation, with some 120,000 grafts being made each year. The Manetti plant, a rosa chinensis hybrid introduced in 1837 by the Botanic Gardens in Milan, Italy, was chosen as the rootstock because it could grow in poor soil and confinement, was extremely hardy, was shade toler-ant and flowered only once in the early summer. This proved to be

Charlie Hotchkiss and Art Clifford, long-time Dale employees, perfected the rose grafting process by rejecting those plants that failed to take, c. 1950. Courtesy R.K. Cooper Collection/RPA

the ideal plant for use in grafting. During the grafting process, a cut was made in the scion, the scion was placed on the Manetti plant with one edge of each plant in contact to allow the sap to flow into the scion and then the graft was string-bound together. Plants that failed to take were picked out by hand. By the time they reached the benches of the rose houses, loss on the grafts averaged about ten percent. They were first kept in an airtight frame from eight to ten days and then gradually exposed to the climate of the houses. Harry Dale's original experimentation on grafting roses had developed into a well organized, perfected operation.

> *Many Brampton children used to go to an area where Dales dumped all of the flowers that did not meet their high standard for selling purposes. On their way home from school, children from across the town would gather bouquets of roses and other flowers, sometimes armfuls, and take them home as "presents" for their mothers. Few houses in Brampton went without Dale flowers, even if they weren't "perfect." In later years, the company discovered that adults were scavenging the flowers and selling them, so the company started shredding all the flowers before they were discarded ... an end to a lovely small town tradition.*

Quality Assurance Increases Sales

Duggan's implementation of grading roses, so key in their operation, needed an overhaul due to the volume of 50,000 roses being harvested on a daily basis. In 1952 a new rose grader was added which was housed in the cool basement of the new addition to the offices and shipping rooms.

An article describes in great depth how the grader worked. *"The purpose of the installation is to obtain uniformity, speed, and to do the grading with minimal handling of the bloom. This is accomplished through using an endless chain on which are fastened "U" shaped hangers designed so that a rose can be quickly slipped on or off without injuring the flower. The first inspection is for the relationship of size of bud and stem length to merit placement in a high grade. The trained eye of the inspector spots those roses not of the highest quality and puts the flower into one of the lower grades. A second inspection is for the straightness*

The roses were graded by length, strength of stalk, and size of bloom. A staff of some 20 women was kept constantly at this task. This 1947 photo was taken before the introduction of the more "high tech" grader installation.
Courtesy R.K. Cooper Collection/RPA

of stem with the crooked necks being eliminated and lifted off the chain. The third inspection removes blooms that are too open, too tight, or with stems with poorly coloured foliage. Once past the checkpoints, the flowers are then graded for size and a final trip checks for any missed imperfections

The roses are kept in water both before and after grading, arriving in randomized bunches, as they are cut in the houses, wrapped in paper and stood in small tanks of water, which are wheeled up to the operators who place each bloom on the hangers. As they are graded, the blooms are wrapped in bunches of twenty-five and again placed with their stems in water. The time for this entire operation is short, insuring the roses are never out of water for more than a minute. Thus, a day's cut of 40,000 to 50,000 roses can be graded in four to five hours."[6]

In 1953 Dales opened up their second wholesale branch office, located in Toronto, the first having been opened in the late '40s in Montreal. Increased business meant increased sales and this enabled the company to provide faster service to the huge Toronto and surrounding markets. The branch office carried a complete line of cut flowers, decorative plants and florist's supplies. They boasted three telephone lines to keep up with their orders. It was reported in the newspaper of the day that, *"By nightfall of opening day the new warehouse and shipping centre was working smoothly. Located right in the city, we can take orders as late as closing time and still get them out that night. Coming from Brampton, these shipments needed another couple or three hours time for transshipping. Here trucks can be loaded inside, under cover, directly from the refrigerator and packing tables."[7]*

Orchids — the Aristocrat of Flowers

The "Orchid Men" took great pride and care in watering each of the over 500,000 orchid plants, c. 1950.
Courtesy Ben Cannons

Not only their famous roses put the Dale name in the forefront as growers of quality flowers, but their world-renowned orchids did as well. These exotic flowers were their second biggest selling item under the direction of Superintendent Parrot. This aristocrat of the flower world drew attention from all visitors as they toured the various greenhouses. All of the men who worked in the orchid houses wore shirts and ties, giving a sense of formality and superiority to the atmosphere surrounding these blooms. One of the men was Harry Cannons who worked for Dales most of his life and found his niche in the growing of orchids. The "Orchid Men" as they were called perfected the hybridization of the orchids in order to increase their stock, size and number of blooms. They were constantly attempting to change and improve upon the colours produced and the growth habits of a particular plant in order to throw strength into the new line.

Pictured here are some of the thousands of orchids that were harvested on a daily basis, c. 1950.
Courtesy RPA

The orchids, of which there were over 200,000 individual plants, continued to solely occupy ten houses on the south side of Rosedale Avenue East, covering approximately one-third of an acre. They grew in moss in pots that stood side by side down rows almost 200 feet in length. The air was kept extremely humid so that drops of water clung to the ceiling and walls and one of the penalties for visitors walking down the rows was to have drops of water down the necks of their shirts. The most popular orchids were the large hybrids, cattleyas, dendrobiums and cymbidiums, ranging in colour from white, mauve, yellow and purple to the more delicate pink, cream and red.

A famous story told many times among the company members and as reported in various newspaper articles of the time, goes as follows, "A *young Toronto bride-to-be sought a large order of white orchids for her wedding. She consulted a Toronto florist who told her that Dales could easily fill the order. But she wanted the very best, which had to come from New York. So the Toronto florist ordered the orchids from New*

York and New York ordered the orchids from Dales. Dales shipped the orchids to New York and they were then shipped back to Toronto to the florist and the young bride paid double duty to assure that she had the very best New York orchids." In another newspaper it was reported that *"The largest orchid order filled by Dales was for the funeral of Chicago gangster Dion O'Bannion. Two hundred and fifty orchid blooms were shipped south by rail."*[8]

A single orchid plant, sometimes taking a lifetime to perfect, was often valued at over $300, c. 1958.
Courtesy RPA

The orchids were tiered for optimum growing conditions which also created a visual delight for visitors to the orchid houses, c. 1958.
Courtesy Douglas Fines

Many of the orchid growers were considered expert or research horticulturists, who devoted themselves to perfecting one of the blooms or plant strains. One employee told a reporter that he had been working for 25 years to perfect the plant he was attending.

As an article of the day reported, *"Such concentrated devotion to the production of a single fragment of beauty in a world in which the atom bomb is stealing all the headlines, is worth recording."*[9]

Brampton — the Centre of the Flower Industry

By the end of 1955, Brampton's population had reached 11,758, doubled from ten years previously. The company added another eight greenhouses to keep up with the demand for their product, bringing their total number of greenhouses to 140. In 1956 they reached their peak production with 20 million blooms cut that year. Of these, half were roses, with the remainder being mums, carnations, tulips, daffodils, orchids, lilies, snapdragons, gardenias, stephanotis, stocks, potted plants, azaleas, hydrangeas, poinsettias, rose bushes, palms, ferns and violets.

The Dale Estate workforce had consolidated at 350 people working in a strong, viable and vibrant business. Many immigrants, upon arrival in Brampton after the war had been sent to the Dale Estate for employment and were subsequently hired. It was well known that there were always jobs to be had at Dales. The newcomers settled into Canadian life, and learned how to grow flowers in the Canadian climate. A number of them left the company and branched out on their own, capitalizing on the knowledge gained while employed at Dales, and Brampton's fame as a flower centre. At this time Brampton boasted a further 12 greenhouse operations, albeit on a small scale, which were scattered across the town.

The Chamber of Commerce promoted Brampton as "The Flower Town of Canada," a recognizable identity for attracting development, c. 1950.
Courtesy RPA

Brampton was earning its reputation as "The Flower Town of Canada," a slogan used by the Chamber of Commerce and various other groups when soliciting business development. The public's demand for flowers had not decreased, and only in hindsight could anyone have predicted what tremendous changes the world would see in the next ten years.

Notes

1. Etheldale Brydon Sivell Collection
2. Harry Letton interview
3. Dale O'Hara Collection
4. *Canadian Growers* Trade Magazine; Dale O'Hara Collection
5. Interview Harry Letton
6. Dale O'Hara Collection
7. Dale O'Hara Collection
8. Interview Etheldale Brydon Sivell
9. *The Conservator*; RPA

Chapter 9

Last of the Small Town Years
1955 — 1960

Noteworthy Events of the Time

1957 Russians launch first satellite into space

1957 Trans-Canada Pipeline completed and natural gas comes to Brampton

1959 Opening of the St. Lawrence Seaway

1959 Opening of "Shoppers World" – Brampton's first indoor shopping mall

1960 Canadian Bill of Rights

I n the mid-1950s, all seemed to be moving along the same way it had since Harry's days during the 1870s. The last greenhouses had been built. The last piece of land had been accumulated. Business had been consolidated but the changing dynamics in the country's economy required new methods of operating. Inventions such as the television were having a profound effect on the way people viewed the world and how they spent their leisure time. Anything that was new was highly desirable; anything old was seen as an unwanted reminder of a past of depression and war. It was clear that the cut flower business needed to keep up with the times by modernizing.

Built on the west side of Main Street in the shadow of the great Dale chimney, these greenhouses were among the last built by the Dale Estate, c.1955.
Courtesy RPA

The New Economy

Tariffs on flowers exported to the United States had been increasing steadily since the 1930s and gradually, shipping its products across the continent was not economically viable for the company. During the mid-50s, the majority of Dale's business was conducted in Canada, for as the population of the country grew, the Canadian market more than picked up any excess capacity which had been lost to the States. To meet the challenge of this new economy, the Dale Estate had a good core of salesmen, such as Cliff Mowat, Johnny Baldock and Bob Johnson, who crossed the country on a regular basis, from Victoria in the West to St. John's in the East. Trips would last as long as six weeks with rail being the main travel choice.

A Sales Awards incentive program was initiated whereby customers could accumulate points redeemable for prizes from the vast stock of Dale flowers or florist's supplies. Florists Conventions sponsored alternately by the Canadian Florist and Growers' Association (CFGA) and Florists Telephone Direct (FTD) were held each year in the main cities, such as Montreal, Winnipeg, Calgary, Edmonton and Halifax, with the Dale Estate leading the membership in size. Florists were a hard-drinking, partying lot who enjoyed many memorable gatherings with friendships being formed across the country.

Fire Strikes

On January 10, 1957, the same year that Brampton reached a population of 13,000, a huge fire broke out in the big boiler room located on the west side of Vodden and Main. Although there had been

$30,000 Fire Hits Dale's Town's Worst Since 1951

Distant Hydrants Hamper Firemen

The most destructive fire to hit Brampton since 1951 roared for three-and-a-half hours through the old boiler room at the Dale Estate on Tuesday afternoon. An estimated $30,000 damage occurred before hard-

In 1957 fire broke out in the boiler room causing extensive damage to the plant and the greenhouses.
Courtesy RPA

minor fires before, this one was particularly destructive. Workmen were dismantling the boiler when the fire broke out, igniting tinder-dry bales of wreath moss. The roof caved in as well as the concrete walls. As soon as the firefighters were able to contain the blaze in the boiler room, emergency crews of steamfitters, glaziers and carpenters went to work making temporary repairs to the ends of five greenhouses to prevent frost from killing the plants inside. Such was the immensity of the fire compared to the small number of hands who were busy fighting it, that no one thought to shut the power off in the corner of the boiler room. Electrical wires carrying 550 volts of electricity remained active but fortunately that part of the huge room was untouched by the fire. The blaze lasted for 3 1/2 hours, cost an estimated $30,000 and, although the greenhouses were saved, the stock damage was extensive. Fire insurance covered part of the damage, but the company had to absorb most of the loss.

Dales Go Retail

In 1957, Dales started a new venture in an attempt to look modern and to capture part of the retail market. To keep up with the trend for drive-in theatres and drive-in hamburger outlets, Dales opened Canada's first drive-in retail flower shop. They had always been a wholesale florist operation but with the increase in local population, they looked for a showplace for their product in an increasingly

sophisticated marketplace. They decided to build a state-of-the-art flower shop, in which to feature the very latest ideas in floral design, to be located in front of the immense boiler room with its huge landmark chimney. Designed in an ultra-modern style with pointed glass façade and natural wooden walls, it epitomized all that was considered desirable in the architecture of the '50s.

Located on the west side of Main Street North, Dale's ultra modern retail store, "Flowerland," opened for business in 1957.
Courtesy C. Chinn Collection/RPA

A press release in the local paper stated, *"The striking modern design has been planned to blend with future landscaping. The large adjoining parking lot should provide convenience for customers and make shopping for flowers, rather than the now customary phone and delivery service, a new and different experience for flower buyers. We are hopeful that not only the people of Brampton will find pleasure in shopping at "Flowerland," but that tourists from all over North America will find it a diverting attraction and at the same time a place where the finest quality of flowers will be available throughout the year."[1]*

New Communities and Enterprises for Brampton

Their optimism was well founded for new industries and businesses were opening up across the town and the county at a highly accelerated rate. Between 1955 and 1960, Brampton annexed almost 4,000 acres under its jurisdiction. The Rice Group built homes, apartment buildings, a shopping mall and a number of industrial buildings, prompting bold headlines in the local paper of, *"Local Building Boom Hits All Time High."* New subdivisions sprang up across the town, such as Eldomar Heights, Northwood Park, Ridgehill Manor and Peel Village to name but a few.

At the same time, a new community, Bramalea, the first of its kind in all of Canada, was being planned to accommodate up to 90,000 people. This self-sufficient satellite community was to cope with the overflow of population from Toronto. A massive undertaking, it called for the building of schools, offices, factories, homes

Bramalea, a satellite community, was constructed east of Brampton and attracted many large industries. This view looking north from the intersection of present-day Steeles Avenue and Dixie Road shows the first housing and industrial development sitting amidst the rolling farmland of the Peel Plain, c. 1957. Courtesy RPA

and stores with house prices being kept at between $20,000 and $30,000 to attract people to the new community. Industries were enticed on the basis of an increased workforce and incentives of inexpensive industrial land; Northern Telecom and the Ford Motor Company were two of the first large enterprises to move to Brampton.

With these tangible earmarks of growth and prosperity, Dale's optimism was well founded. They continued to win prizes at international and national flower shows. A newspaper reported, *"For many years wherever the firm has exhibited, the winning ribbon has been brought home. Each year at the Canadian National Exhibition and at the Royal Winter Fair held in Toronto, the Dale Estate shows a large and non-competitive display of its best floriculture specimens. It is indicative of the modesty and thought for the industry as a whole that the Dale Estate during the past few years has not entered flower shows in an effort to encourage other growers to win laurels. This hasn't stemmed the ardour for experiment however for the Dale Botanical Department has continued to develop new varieties of roses, among them the famed Rosedale, Dorothy Dale, Sunbeam and the most recent that attracted public attention, the Ida Costain rose named after the wife of the great Canadian historical novelist."*[2]

Sarah Dale Algie, on the right, is shown presenting Ida Costain, wife of noted Canadian author, Thomas B. Costain, (seated to the left) a bouquet of the roses the Dale Estate developed in her honour, c. 1958.
Courtesy C. Chinn Collection/RPA

The firm at this time declared its production figures in the local newspaper as: 40 acres of greenhouses and buildings; 1.5 million square feet of glass; 20 million blooms produced each year, of which 9 million were roses, 2 million carnations, 1.5 million chrysanthemums, 2 million tulips, daffodils and other bulb stock, 100 thousand orchids, 150 thousand lilies; as well as assorted thousands of snapdragons, stocks, sweet peas, etc.

Dales Keeps Pace and Popularity

In 1957, W.A. Beatty retired from the day-to-day operations of the company, taking over the position as President of the Board of Directors from Sarah Dale Algie, with Douglas Dickson, Ethel Dale

Brydon's son-in-law, named as Executive Vice-President. Dales maintained its family atmosphere as employee picnics, dances and various social events were held on a yearly basis.

The wages at Dales continued to be very low as evidenced by one secretary, Florence Mowat, who made $33 a week. This was on a par with most of the older industries of Brampton such as Hewetsons, but well below the average wages which were $10 to $15 higher in the newer businesses. Although the salary was low, it was offset by the fact that the business was stable and no one was ever fired.[3]

Tony Stapleton, shipper, and Abbie Hilgartner, packer, are pictured in Dale's shipping room, c. 1960. Courtesy Glynne Everson

As one former employee, Glynne Everson said, *"Other companies would lay off, fire or go bankrupt but at Dales you always knew that you had a job for life … sort of like a big family."* Working at Dales was also a clean job unlike many of the factory jobs in the area. When speaking about the working conditions of the time, Glynne Everson described them as, *"Most of the employees worked seven days a week with Saturday and Sunday afternoons off. All people came in on Sunday morning to cut the flowers. The duty man worked Saturday and Sunday taking turns to keep the temperatures right in the greenhouses. Also night pipers were always on duty to keep the temperatures right with the steam heat. In the '50s Dales started to pay them time and a half overtime for this work. At the end of every year, the men would get their pay raises, from two to five cents an hour depending on how management felt. I would call off their name and the raise would be awarded.*

Jim Algie, son of Sarah Dale Algie, worked in the accounting department of the Dale Estate, c. 1960.
Courtesy Glynne Everson

The weekly payroll was about $17,000. Jim Algie and I would go to the TD Bank at the corner of Main and Queen, pick it up in cash, wait for the police chief, who

would follow us in his car back to Dales. We would then spend two hours putting each amount in cash in the employee pay envelope. Income tax, Blue Cross and Canada Savings Bond were the only deductions. Because the business was deemed agricultural, no unemployment insurance was deducted. However, Dales footed the bill for the interest free loan on the purchases of the CSB. One of the men got sick and on the advice of his doctor he was supposed to take a six-month leave of absence. Dales advanced him his pay and held his job for him. Dales also gave garden space to employees on the land known as the Flats beside the Etobicoke Creek. Each plot measured approximately 50 x 100 and each year the company would rototill and fertilize the plots. I know I worked too long hours for little pay but I loved working for Dales."[4]

In a further interview with Florence Mowat she stated, *"I worked from 8 a.m. until 6 p.m. every day and then in peak times, sometimes until midnight. We had no official breaks as the morning was always a big rush to meet the trucks and the 10:16 a.m. train to Toronto. We could always go to the shipping department and get an arrangement or a bouquet of flowers. I remember one day I was wearing an artificial brooch and Mr. Beatty asked me what was that on my dress and I told him it was an artificial flower that my aunt had given me. Well, Mr. Beatty took me down to the shipping department to Harry Morris and told him that from then on I was to have a fresh bouquet of flowers on my desk every day and a fresh corsage for my dress, and there was!"*[5]

Dales continued to use trucks in local deliveries with between eight and ten trucks in their fleet at any one time. There were daily deliveries to Niagara, Kitchener, Owen Sound and Toronto and two trucks called "load luggers" that hauled the soil and peat moss around to the numerous greenhouses, which were each divided into various ranges with their own person in charge. Harry Letton, who had started working at Dales in 1926, recalled the names of those in charge. *"I looked after the azaleas, the poinsettias and the hydrangeas; Art Bradly did the cyclamens; Davie McCanless the begonias, Alfie Hoff the asparagus; Baldy Ewles the violets; George Wilson the potted roses; and Dick Smith*

A Dale Estate truck idles in winter while waiting to load the day's shipment of flowers, c. 1960. Courtesy Glynne Everson

and John Osborne the exotic plants.[6] Harry left Dales in the mid-1950s to work at a higher-paying job in Malton but still remembered his years working at Dales with great affection.

Roses for the Stratford Festival

A further effort to consolidate their market and enhance their reputation led to the inauguration of a delightful tradition that continued for several years. In conjunction with *The Toronto Telegram*, Dales sponsored a train that ran to the newly opened Stratford Festival Theatre in Stratford, Ontario. Tickets were sold for a Festival Train

A Dale Rose was given to each lady who boarded the "Tely Train" to the Stratford Festival, c. 1958. Courtesy RPA

that left Toronto, stopped in Brampton to pick up passengers and Dale Estate personnel, included a dinner in a Stratford church, a bus to the Festival Theatre, and then the train ride back to Toronto. One woman recalled, *"I remember clearly the train stopping in Brampton and a young girl coming down the aisle of the train handing each of the ladies a lovely long stemmed red rose compliments of the Dale Estate. On one of the leaves was the name DALE. It was so elegant and made us feel very special."* This annual event was sold out well in advance and the gift of a Dale Autographed Rose became a fond memory for years after the Festival Train's demise.

"Nature Walk" Tours for Charity

In 1958, a much-publicized and popular event was *The Telegram* "Nature Walk" Tours of the Dale Estate, pairing with the Brampton Rotary Club and the Brampton Chapter of the Victorian Order of Nurses to raise money for charity. For several years, in the late winter months, Dales opened its greenhouses for charity tours. People from Toronto and the surrounding area came by the busloads, waiting patiently in line for up to four hours to get a look at the abundance of flowers. Newspaper accounts of the day estimated

In 1958, tours of the Dale greenhouses attracted thousands of visitors to see and photograph the acres of flowers.
Courtesy C. Chinn Collection/RPA

crowds as large as 10,000 per day, necessitating opening the greenhouses for additional days of touring. Amateur photographers were encouraged to take pictures but discouraged from picking the flowers, in particular the orchids! All proceeds from these tours went to the Rotary Club who had two shows on the Sundays in February and March in aid of Camp Ro-bogi and the VON who had two camera days in March. Many visitors in later years remember the smell of the roses, the high humidity of the orchid houses and the seemingly miles and miles of greenhouses.

The End of Small Town Brampton

As the end of the decade drew near, the flowers continued to be grown and held in high esteem across Canada and the continent as a symbol of quality and excellence. However, small town Brampton had ceased to exist. Immigrants from around the world, in particular Portugal, The Netherlands, Germany and the British Isles, arrived and altered Brampton's racial mix. The confines of the once static, staid and solidly British town were bursting at the seams with the population exploding to 24,363 in 1961, almost double that of ten years previously. In order to build offices and factories and to accommodate housing for this increased population, Brampton had annexed farmland, making the town twice the size it had been when first incorporated and necessitating major changes to its infrastructure.

Water now came from Lake Ontario instead of local wells and electricity was transported mainly underground. The sewage system became greatly overworked necessitating a revamping of waste treatment. Overcrowding of the existing schools triggered a building boom for the Peel Board of Education. Peel Memorial Hospital was also overcrowded and began to expand yet again. The Trans-Canada pipeline came through town bringing inexpensive natural gas to homes that previously had to rely on either coal or oil for fuel. Shoppers World, Brampton's first indoor shopping mall, opened for business at the corner of Steeles and Hurontario. Large industries such as American Motors Auto Manufacturer located in Brampton and each of these required a significant workforce, offering well-paid, unionized jobs. Little Brampton was barely recognizable under the buzz and hum of prosperity.

Decreased Profit for Dales

While others were prospering in the burgeoning economy, the Dale Estate began to find it increasingly difficult to earn a profit, despite their attempts to modernize their business. This had its origin in many factors that had slowly been at work since shortly after the war. From just a handful of florists in the town of Brampton in the 1940s, there were 48 nurseries listed in 1961. Each of these small family-run nurseries were selling flowers to the general public, flooding the market, and Dale's floral business was no longer the only game in town.

However, one of the biggest factors resulting in decreased profits for the company was the rising price of oil. Having converted their seven huge coal-fired boilers to oil just a scant ten years prior, this supposed cost-saving conversion was proving to be an ever-increasing drain on the operating costs of the company, as the demand for oil, and hence oil prices, started to dramatically rise. Thought was given to converting to the cheaper natural gas that had come to town but this proved to be a financially impossible consideration.

Another factor was trying to replace the aging Dale workforce, most of whom had begun their working career at Dales in the 1920s

Pictured in the shipping room are long time Dale employees (l to r) Tony Stapleton; shipper, Abbie Hilgartner; packer, Aubrey Patton; packer, and sitting is Bill Goddard; packer, c. 1960. Courtesy Glynne Everson

and were now approaching retirement age. Young men were loath to enter an industry that required long hours with no benefits, for Dales did not have a union or a pension plan. The wage scale was very low although they did pay more than most of the other florists in town, but for young men with families, jobs at union scale with full benefits were plentiful at the new local industrial giants such as Northern Electric. Many of the Dale Estate company men had spent their lifetime perfecting the growing of the exquisite roses, orchids, chrysanthemums and carnations that had made Dales famous throughout the conti-nent. With fewer young men willing to enter the business, much of the growing expertise that had made Dales successful was being lost.

A Dale's truck delivers flowers directly to the waiting TCA plane at Malton Airport for shipment to distant markets, c. 1962. Courtesy Jim Taylor Collection

The face of transportation was also dramatically changing. Where there had been over 20 trains a day taking flowers to the heart of the continent, there were now just 10, served by only one railway line the CNR, the CPR having ended commercial transportation that had serviced Brampton for almost a century. In order for the Dale Estate to fulfill their mandate of prompt same day service, ensuring the highest quality of stock, it became necessary to ship mostly by air and truck transport, although some product was still shipped by train. This led to a dramatic escalation in shipping costs due to the increasing rise in fuel prices.

Added to this was the fact that whatever could be shipped out quickly to the marketplace by air, could also be shipped in. The market began to be flooded with cheaper flowers grown in the milder climates of Europe and Central America and flown in fresh to places such as Brampton. These countries had lower labour costs and hence could readily absorb the higher costs of air transport.

A teenage Dale Dickson O'Hara is pictured among the exotic Dale Estate orchids.
Courtesy Dale O'Hara Collection/ photograph by Russ Cooper

Despite the fact that these flowers were of lesser quality than what Dales produced, the consumer became less discerning, preferring ready, cheap quantity to quality. Coupled with this was the fact that plastic, developed during the Second World War, had invaded the flower market. Consumers could now purchase life-like flowers to decorate their homes and business environments at a fraction of the cost of fresh flowers. Plastic flower arrangements were non-perishable and were seen by the consumer as a cheap method of decoration. Soon cut flowers became only a special occasion purchase at Christmas, Easter, Mother's Day and funerals. Further undermining the cut flower trade was a newcomer to the florist industry. Grocery stores started cutting into the floral market as food chains, such as Loblaws, consolidated into large emporiums offering more than just food. They began selling flowers and houseplants at cut-rate prices, starting the trend to one-stop shopping.

Capital Needed to Survive

The economics of rising oil prices, air transportation, plastic flowers and additional floral outlets had radically changed the face of the economy for florists, and Dales could no longer compete. After watching their decreasing profitability, it was apparent that the company required a large infusion of cash to keep the business operational. This much-needed capital was required in order to

This aerial view of the intersection of Main and Vodden streets shows the vast number of greenhouses that dominated the landscape of Brampton, c. 1955.
Courtesy RPA

upgrade the facility as some of the greenhouses and heating pipes were over 100 years old and in serious need of modernization. Cash was required to attract a younger workforce for it was getting harder and harder to find reliable, loyal employees at the lower wages. A solution was to mechanize the methods of growing and to offer better working conditions. All of this modernization required additional capital.

The Dale family had to make a difficult decision. They could keep the status quo with the consequences being to have their incomes slowly erode as profits continued to slide. Within this family-owned business, the Dale descendants, including Harry's one remaining daughter, Sarah, and many of his grandchildren, shared in the ever-shrinking profits of the Dale Estate. There was a distinct possibility that without the increase in cash to offset the economic realities of the time, the company would soon go bankrupt. The second option was to find a buyer, one who would invest in the assets and reputation of the Dale Estate, thus keeping afloat the company for not only the continued growth of their beloved roses, but also for the benefit of the remaining loyal employees.

DALE ESTATE IS SOLD

The Company is Sold

The sale of the Dale Estate in 1961 prompted shock in the small town of Brampton as evidenced by the bold headlines in the local papers.

Courtesy Dale O'Hara Collection

The family decided to sell. On October 19, 1961, the company, founded so lovingly by Harry Dale, ceased to be a family business and was sold to Federal Farms Inc., a division of the Weston family of companies. The news came as a surprise to the citizens of the town for Dales had been such a solid fixture since its inception that almost everyone knew someone, or had themselves been involved, in the business. The Dale Estate represented their past, their stability and their identity as "The Flower Town of Canada." With all other Brampton institutions undergoing rapid change, this was just one more unsettling shift in their everyday lives. The townspeople were shocked when bold, two-inch headlines screamed across the daily paper "*DALE ESTATE IS SOLD*".

The lead article of the day stated, "*The Dale Estate Ltd. has been purchased by Federal Farms Inc. of Bradford, and other Canadian interests, it was announced last Tuesday. Confirmation of the purchase was made,*

Douglas Dickson, vice-president under the new management, carries on the day-to-day business of promoting the quality and excellence of the Dale flowers, c. 1961. Courtesy Jim Taylor Collection

following Toronto Stock Exchange approval, by Philip Latchman, president of Federal Farms Inc., growers and purveyors of fresh vegetables. The sale price was not announced. Mr. Latchman said 'Operation of the company will be revamped and new methods of merchandising introduced to strengthen its marketing program. The company's scope will be substantially enlarged in a carefully programmed expansion.' In addition to the many types of flowers and plants the firm currently grows, the new management is considering growing and marketing hothouse vegetables. Operations will be under the full management of Federal Farms. W.A. Beatty and Douglas Dickson, Dale directors for many years, will continue as directors. New directors appointed include, Philip Latchman, Morrie Latchman, vice-president and general manager of Federal Farms, Douglas R. Annett, president of Annett and Co. Ltd. and Carman G. King, director of Annett and Co. Mr. Beatty has been elected chairman of the board, Morrie Latchman, president and Douglas Dickson, vice-president."[7]

Under the sales agreement, the family received $1.6 million, which was divided among Harry Dale's direct heirs and, as most were deceased, in turn their beneficiaries. The family felt saddened, yet satisfied, secure in the knowledge that the firm would carry on, flowers would still be grown, and employment for the 300 plus employees would continue.

For almost a century the Dale Estate was known across the continent for the quality of its flowers as evidenced by this collection of medals won at international flower competitions. Courtesy Virginia Gould Collection/Photograph by Finn O'Hara

Notes

1. *The Conservator*; RPA
2. *The Conservator*; RPA
3. Interview Florence and Cliff Mowat
4. Interview Glynne Everson
5. Interview Florence Mowat
6. Interview Harry Letton
7. *The Times and Conservator*; RPA

Chapter 10

The Decline of Brampton's Floral Industry
1960 — 1970

Noteworthy Events of the Time

1961 USA involved in Vietnam War

1962 Trans-Canada Highway completed

1964 Canada Flag Act

1968 Trudeau becomes leader of Liberal Party and Prime Minister

1969 USA lands the first man on the moon

1968-1973 Inflation at 7.5% per annum

1970 War Measures Act put into effect to combat Quebec Terrorism

I n February 1962, the Dale Estate became a publicly-owned company listed on the Toronto Stock Exchange with an opening offering of $3.50 per share. Trading was brisk with over 3,000 shares being sold on the first day. Many employees, some of whom had been with Dales for years, put their life savings into the new company, such was their loyalty and trust.

Federal Farms

Federal Farms, the holding company for the Dale Estate, was described in a prospectus of the time, as having $27 million in assets. Incorporated in 1948, the company controlled 440 acres of choice farmland in the Holland Marsh area with highly-integrated growing and marketing facilities. Its subsidiaries included Bradford Cooling Co., which featured the quick cooling of leaf vegetables. Federal Farms had shown a profit every year since its inception, including 1961 when it reported $28,000 net profit. It appeared to all concerned that the Dale Estate had found a perfect match. Federal Farms appeared to be a company with enough money to help in Dale's restructuring, a company with a fresh outlook on marketing, which understood the nature of the business and could marry the sale of flowers with their products. After all, they had access to the Weston Group, Loblaws, and their own grocery stores to tap into the new market for selling flowers.

Under New Management

Federal Farms was to assume management of the company for a period of ten years, and they started immediately with a management shake-up and a change in business practices. As stated in a news release, *"The company will display more versatility in production. Without sacrificing flower production, the company will put unused*

greenhouse space to work, producing hot-house vegetables. At the same time production methods will be organized so that flower and plant production can be increased while the same high quality of the Dale product is maintained." [1]

Playing a leading role in the new productivity was Harry Dale Jr., grand-son of William Dale and great-nephew of the elder Harry Dale. Latchman, the president of the company, appointed Harry Jr., who had a B.Sc. in agriculture with a major in floriculture from the University of Guelph, as Vice-President of Production. After 25 years at Dales, Harry Jr. had left the company and had moved to Calgary to work as manager of Tyrell's Flowers Limited. During his years with Dales, Harry had become an expert in the production end of the business by working for three years in various capacities of production at the growing level, progressing through the soils laboratory and finally becoming general superin-tendent. He had served many terms in associations, such as the Ontario Division of Allied Florists and Growers of Canada, Roses Inc. and the International Association of Commercial Rose Growers. Because of the retirement of most of the senior growers at Dales, Latchman had enticed Harry Jr. back to Dales to ensure the continua-tion of the high quality production of the flowers.

The Flower Festival of Brampton

As part of a new marketing strategy for the Dale Estate, the Flower Festival of Brampton was inaugurated in 1963 as the Town struggled

to maintain its identity as "The Flower Town of Canada." Because of Brampton's 48 growers, including the Dale Estate with its history for drawing tourists to its greenhouses, it seemed logical to promote the Town and the company by patterning the Festival after the giant Portland Rose Festival in the United States. The Dale Estate in conjunction with the Brampton Chamber of Commerce created

Floral displays, flower shows and exhibits were just some of the many events at the Festival of Flowers, 1966. Courtesy C. Chinn Collection/RPA

the Brampton Festival of Flowers Association, formed various committees and, after many months of planning, held the first Festival on June 28 to July 1, 1963. An advertising brochure proclaimed, *"Stratford has its Shakespearean Festival — Toronto its Canadian National Exhibition — Calgary its Stampede. Now, let's make Brampton famous from coast to coast as the home of Canada's Annual Festival of Flowers. It's a big undertaking. It needs the enthusiastic support and co-operation of every citizen. Talk it up.*

The 1966 Flower Festival Queen, Jean Bull, with a bouquet of Dale Roses.
Courtesy C. Chinn Collection/RPA

The Decline of Brampton's Floral Industry   129

Tell and write your friends about it. Start now to plant flowers and beautify your home and grounds. Help make Brampton a place of beauty when Festival Days roll round."[2] There was a Grand Floral Parade, a flower show, sports activities, a flower queen contest, special church services, art exhibits, musical presentations, film presentations, and projects for the further beautification of home and industry. The lofty ideals of community improvement through the flower industry, both socially and physically bore fruit for the next dozen years, until the nurseries that had made Brampton so famous unfortunately completely disappeared.

Brampton's Real Estate Boom

Brampton continued to grow at a phenomenal rate. In just a scant two years, from 1962 to 1964, the population increased by 10,000. Industrial land was being gobbled up with new businesses and industries seeming to open every day. In the town real estate market, business was exceptionally brisk as stated in the annual report, *"Sales for 1964 total $2,433,570 as compared to a 1963 level of $1,695,960, an increase of 44% with sales for 1965 predicted to be even higher."*[3] More than 700 building permits were issued in 1964 for a total construction cost value of more than $18 million. Real estate had become the new currency with available land becoming highly desirable. The employment situation was excellent with only 2.7 percent of the total Brampton labour force unemployed, 1 percent lower than the national unemployment level.

Acquisitions and Takeovers

By the middle of the decade, Federal Farms soon realized that the problems encountered by Dales, namely a diminishing return on the products produced, were not as easily overcome as anticipated. Their various retail ventures proved to be unprofitable as customers were more inclined to shop in the new indoor malls and, with cheap plastic and grocery store discounted flowers, few were buying quality roses. Despite various marketing and advertising initiatives, sales could not keep pace with production costs. The much-needed repair and modernization of the facility failed to take place and Federal Farms looked elsewhere to acquire assets to prop up their investment. In 1964 they bought McKinney Wholesale of Montreal for $4 million, changing the name to Dale McKinney Co., and continued to look around for other companies to acquire.

W.E. Calvert Ltd. of Brampton, although not in the same category size-wise as the Dale Estate, had over the years become a profitable, well-known and respected grower. In his early years Walter Calvert had saved enough money to purchase land north of the Dale Estate. While working at Dales as a young man, he had built his own greenhouse and, so the story goes, started his seedlings under the Dale Estate flower benches. He hired men from Dales who wished to moonlight and, once established, he eventually branched out on his own. With the help of his wife Ada, who made the rounds of the local retailers, he sold not only his own flowers but also the wholesale flowers purchased from Dales. Walter offered flowers of the highest quality and eventually became a specialist in the growing of chrysanthemums. Being canny enough to neither try to compete with the growing of the Dale roses nor with the loyalty of the employees, he was able to carve out a niche for himself. Walter successfully started the first consortium by having consignment agreements with local growers and other smaller nurseries, and over the years expanded his acreage and greenhouses. In 1959 Calverts made a large capital expenditure and built a modern facility and new greenhouses totalling 25,000 square feet under glass, which accounted for 20 percent of the total company production. In 1964 they were selling 3,500 pots of chrysanthemums per week and under the direction of Walter's son Jack, Calverts employed 123 men. It was a family-run business, which included sons and brothers-in-law, all of whom had a direct hand in the daily management of the company.

Calvert's size, location and success came to the attention of Federal Farms and, despite vigorous and vehement protests from management within the

The demand for quality roses such as these displayed in the '50s by W.A.Beatty and John Beatty (no relation) began to decrease in the mid '60s. Courtesy R.K. Cooper Collection /RPA

The Calvert greenhouses, numbering just over 21 with an additional 25 acres of open cultivation, occupied the land north and west of Archibald and Main, c. 1960. Courtesy R.K. Cooper Collection /RPA

The Decline of Brampton's Floral Industry   131

Dale Estate and its wholesale houses, the takeover bid began. In 1965 Federal Farms purchased W.E. Calvert Ltd. for $1 million, almost the same purchase price as for the Dale Estate five years earlier, an indication of the rapidly rising cost of living. The two companies together would produce 20 percent of the total wholesale value of all flowers grown for commercial purposes in Canada and about 33 percent of those grown in Ontario. The agreement provided for the purchase by the Dale Estate Ltd. of all operating assets of W. E. Calvert Ltd. including their land, buildings, plant, equipment, inventories and accounts receivable, but excluding the family homes. Calverts were paid $500,000 in cash and held a mortgage for the remainder of the funds, which was to be paid over a ten-year period. The majority of the funds were derived from the British Mortgage and Trust Co. and the remainder from other bank sources.

New Company Formed

The sale was completed and the two firms were merged. Jack, who had control of the Calvert company, made only one stipulation in order for the sale to go ahead — that the name Calvert be retained and become first in any merged company entity. Illogical as this may have seemed, as it was the Dale Estate who had the more recognizable logo, the new firm became known as the Calvert-Dale Estate. There had always been a petty small town rivalry between the two companies and management from the old firm, for the most part nearing retirement, declined to work under the direction of the Calverts. The last continuous family connections to the Dale business, begun almost a century earlier by Edward and Harry Dale, ended with the merger of the two firms.

The 1965 merger of the two firms created the largest greenhouse operation of its kind in Canada. Courtesy RPA

A small note that should have sent alarm bells ringing throughout the two companies was that surplus vacant land owned by Calverts was immediately put up for sale, the proceeds of which were to be used to pay down the mortgage held by the banks and the Calvert family.

The Calvert-Dale Estate Ltd.

The Calvert-Dale Estate listed their production as follows:
– 6.7 million roses,
– 2 million sweetheart roses,
– 3 million snapdragons,
– 5 million chrysanthemums and pompoms,
– Greenhouses covering 40 acres,
– 1,800,000 square feet of glass,
– 25,000 square feet of cold storage space,
– 573 employees,
– Three wholesale establishments, namely the original Montreal-Dale Branch, the acquired Dale McKinney Co. and the Toronto-Dale Branch.

Courtesy C. Chinn Collection/RPA

In the progress report filed by Federal Farms on November 22, 1965, the Board of Directors painted a rosy financial picture, *"The stock at today's prices ($2.20 – $2.25) has good speculative value, minimal downside risk and the potential of doubling in price over the next few years."*[4] They claimed that increased profits were due to the introduction of certain efficiencies, namely lower production and marketing costs, but in fact it was due to offsetting the losses from one company by taking the profits of the other. In the spring of 1965, just a scant six months after the takeover, shareholders were told they could expect earnings of $200,000 or 30 cents a share. Also, by adding a two percent increase in their prices and a proposed new carbon dioxide process to enhance growing conditions in the greenhouses, the earnings might be raised to $325,000 or 51 cents per share.

A Rosy Future Painted

Under their future prospects the annual report stated: *"New management has launched a drive for higher efficiencies and greater productivity. The marketing operation has already shown a great improvement. Flowers are shipped within 48 hours of being cut, improving the quality and eliminating high inventories and waste. More can be accomplished; the company is working towards adjusting the production to meet market demand and scheduling an even, year round production, supplementing the peak periods. The old Dale company had been poor in scheduling, unable to meet peak demand when prices were relatively high and because of surpluses, forced to dump during the summer. Price structure will be investigated. There has been no increase in the average annual price of wholesale cut flowers for over 20 years and by increasing the price by 1%, it would add increased pre-tax earnings without the need for any increase in sales. To increase production, attention has been focused on improving productivity rather than enlarging facilities."*[5]

Under Jack Calvert's direction, improved productivity was to take two directions. First was to revitalize the greenhouses by laying tiles to allow adequate drainage, soil sterilization and proper balanced

fertilizing. The second was the introduction of polyethylene ducts and 18 carbon-dioxide-producing units at a cost of $22,000, which was a substantial outlay as it represented half their yearly profit. The report claimed that this method would increase production of mums and roses with larger stems and bigger flowers by between 10 and 20 percent. They estimated the increase in production without the addition of increased greenhouse capacity would result in about $500,000 in additional sales or $165,000 in earnings per year.

The last item the report mentions is the sale of land. *"The sale of premium, surplus land is being successfully pursued and the proceeds will retire some of the high interest-bearing debt from the purchase of Calverts by Federal Farms. It is anticipated this will save $30,000 per year in interest charges."*[6] In the

Jack Calvert is shown in the greenhouses of the Calvert-Dale Estates Ltd, c. 1965.
Courtesy Calvert Collection/ RPA

President's report of the same year, Jack Calvert stated *"The company is continuing its policy of disposing of land not essential to its operations. Total land sales amounted to $335,710."*[7] This was the first indication of what eventually would become the total collapse of the floral industry in Brampton.

A winter view of the greenhouse ranges in the "flats" looking east toward the Etobicoke Creek. Harsh weather conditions were a constant concern in the floral industry, c. 1964.
Courtesy Glynne Everson

The Decline Becomes Evident

Beneath all of the annual report rhetoric was a startling fact. The combined company production of both Calvert's and Dale's at this time was a mere 20 million blooms, the same number of blooms that the Dale Estate alone had produced ten years earlier in 1956. It was apparent that the domestic floral industry was dying.

New management started to take over the running of the Calvert-Dale company, with William Walker C.A. joining the firm as controller to take charge of all accounting and office management. By December of the same year, 1965, the interim report to shareholders laid the blame for poor production on "the worst growing weather on record throughout the Fall months," a factor that had always been common in the flower industry. In the same year, the company began to put its modernization plan into action by making considerable capital expenditures. The Toronto-Dale branch office was moved to a more modern location, flower benches and greenhouses got a facelift and the carbon dioxide gas equipment, originally estimated to cost $22,000, was installed for a capital expenditure in excess of $110,000. Shareholders were also apprised that high growing expenses were incurred during the first six months of the year but flowers were mainly produced in the latter six months of the year. Streamlined production and scheduling of the huge flower enterprise was not quite as easy as first anticipated

Carnations, which were easier to grow, began to supplant the Dale roses. In this photo, taken at the former Calvert plant, are some of the women employed in preparing the carnations for shipment. Courtesy Calvert Collection/RPA

by the management team under Jack Calvert. However, in 1966 the company continued to remain optimistic and Calvert was confident that the previous year's earnings would be surpassed. This was not the case and in 1967, a loss of $198,909 was reported, followed in 1968 by a loss of $212, 745.

In various interviews it was stated that the company began to devolve into organized chaos.[8] Carnations, a Calvert specialty, started to supplant the famous Dale roses for carnations were cheaper and easier to grow, requiring less care and a cooler environment. This translated into savings on heat and labour, as fewer men were required to tend the carnations, the so-called "poor man's rose." Gradually the expertise required for growing roses was lost with the older generation gone and little commitment to the art from those left behind. The florist supply side of the business, which had developed into a major source of revenue for the company, was scattered between five operations and was no longer profitable or efficient. New staff from other growing operations was hired, such as Bill Waters from Waters Florists, in an attempt to bring in new ideas and solve the ever-increasing loss of profit. With the influx of new personnel, the concept of a family run business with all of its inherent loyalties and shared history had finally been irreparably broken.

In 1967, after a disastrous Easter production where the lilies did not open on time and thus missed the marketplace, Roy Nicholson was brought on to the Board of Directors.

"Last-Ditch" Efforts

In 1968, with profits, production and sales falling while expenditures were rising, the Board of Directors of the Calvert-Dale Estate removed Jack Calvert from his position with the company and subsequently all of his family.[9] Nicholson, who had a background in the florist industry, became president and under his direction, the company was gradually dismantled. Competitors, smelling blood, started to chip away at the company and hire away disgruntled employees. In the annual report to the shareholders in 1968, the company outlined the grave situation, namely that there was a loss in operations of $198,561, and a decline in sales of florist supplies of $102,000. Their selling and distribution costs had increased 15 percent due to wage increases and the expansion of the company's branch outlets and selling routes to London and Ottawa, Ontario. They announced that the management staff of the existing branches in Montreal and Toronto had been replaced and a new person, W.J. Corrigan, was hired and placed in charge of distribution.

Despite all of the losses incurred, the company opened a small retail branch in the Shoppers World Mall in Brampton, closing their flagship store, Flowerland, which had opened with such high hopes just ten years prior. In the same report, the company explained that capital expenditures were high due to the installation of a new steam line in order to eliminate two boiler rooms, the necessity for replacements and additions to the delivery truck fleet and leasehold improvements at the new branch and retail outlets. They also claimed that working capital continued to be depleted by long-term debt payments necessitating incurring a debenture of $300,000.

In the late 1960s, many of the older Dale greenhouses were uneconomical to operate and beyond repair and consequently were abandoned. Courtesy Iris Tuckey

A final note in the report was the most telling for the future of the company. They reported that uneconomic greenhouse area, totaling 300,000 square feet, was permanently closed. The roses were abandoned. The heat was turned off. The men were let go. The greenhouses rapidly fell into disrepair and their once magnificent infrastructure collapsed. The company proceeded to employ a consultant to develop a long-range plan for its properties, particularly those that would become surplus to operations. This plan was to be presented to the Brampton Town Council to *"facilitate the orderly integration of some of the company's properties into the overall town planning."*[10]

It was apparent that the company was no longer a floral industry, but was now mainly in the business of property development, seeking Town approval for the development of houses and retail space.

Notes

1. *The Conservator;* RPA
2. *Brampton's 100th Anniversary Book*
3. *The Times and Conservator;* RPA
4. Calvert Collection; RPA
5. Calvert Collection; RPA
6. Calvert Collection; RPA
7. Calvert Collection; RPA
8. Interview Bill Waters
9. Calvert Collection; RPA
10. Calvert Collection; RPA

Chapter 11

Demise of the Dale Estate
1970 — 1980

Noteworthy Events of the Time

1972-73 Watergate unfolds in USA/ Richard Nixon resigns as president

1973-74 OPEC raises price of oil leading to "oilflation"

1974 Creation of Regional Government and City of Brampton

1975 Vietnam War ends with complete withdrawal of USA forces

1975 CN Tower completed

1975 Wage and Price Controls in effect across Canada

1979-1982 Worldwide recession

In 1971, the company claimed a small operating profit but production continued to decrease, necessitating the purchase of flowers from outside sources. This, coupled with the cost of paying the interest on the debt incurred by acquisitions, crippled their working capital, with the florist supply end of the business being the only profitable part of the company. The Town of Brampton was in the final stage of granting rezoning of the Dale Estate and Calvert land for family housing and it appeared that the true assets of the company were not in the flowers but in the land on which the acres of greenhouses sat.

In 1972 moderate profits were made mainly from the Montreal operation, the florist supply end of the business, the increase in sales of imported lilies and hydrangeas for the Easter market, plus the reduced costs resulting from the greatly-diminished production of roses. Despite the profit, however, the company continued to be plagued by a working capital problem, and a further debenture of $200,000 was issued.

First Block of Land Sold

The Town Council approved the re-development plan proposed by the Calvert-Dale Estate, and it released 6.7 acres at the corner of Main and Vodden streets for development in 1972. A company report stated, *"The greenhouses on this property are the oldest of the company's ranges and are beyond repair. The loss of these greenhouses will substantially reduce the productive capacity of the company."*[1] The accounting firm of Stewart Young and Mason Ltd. placed a market value of $4,335,000 on property valued just six months prior at $1,499,028. In 1973, the shareholders approved an agreement that provided for the sale of the first block of land to a development company, and granted an option on most of the company's land in

Current view of the busy intersection of Main and Vodden streets where Harry Dale's home and greenhouses once stood, 2007. Courtesy Dale O'Hara Collection

Brampton for development over a period of time. Under the agreement, 35 percent of the greenhouses would be phased out by the end of the year.

To make up for the lack of their own production, the company planned to purchase their flowers from other growers as well as the recently formed Flower Auction in Malton. This would allow the wholesale flower and florist supply divisions to continue. Improvement in roadways into the heart of Brampton, the most notable being the 401 and 410 extensions, enabled the company to close its Toronto wholesale branch in an attempt to further reduce costs. Philip Latchman, the remaining representative of Federal Farms, retired and was replaced by Jack Kaufman, President of A.L. Randall Co. With these dramatic changes in the structure of the company, and with the infusion of cash from the sale of land, the company limped towards the middle of the decade, a mere shadow of its former glory.

Further Losses

In 1975, the company experienced great losses with the major reason being the escalating cost of fuel oil. It took 3 million gallons of oil per year at an estimated cost of $1 million to heat their remaining greenhouses. These houses, mostly built in the '30s and '40s, were old and uneconomical to operate, as roses required high humidity and heat to grow properly. A further reason was the rapidly rising cost of labour. Eighty percent of overhead expenses was directly related to these costs and for a company that was built on cheap wages and low fuel costs in a cold climate, these two factors undermined any further chance the company had at profitability.

In a letter to the shareholders on November 14, 1975, the company reported, "*As a direct result of increases in the cost of fuel oil and labour, and with no relief in the foreseeable future, the company has decided to phase out and close down the major portions of its greenhouses, and is now in the process of phasing them out. The greenhouses will be sold for salvage. Roses will continue to be grown at the range known as Calvert Plant no. 1, a greenhouse area of 100,000 square feet which has its own heating plant."*[2]

The Floral Industry in Name Only

All of the Dale greenhouses that had been built over the years from 1870 to 1956, establishing the largest floral operation on the continent, were to be demolished. Employees were given eight weeks notice terminating their employment and, while the company continued to purchase flowers from outside sources, the Calvert-Dale Estate remained a flower industry in name only. The new assistant general manager, George Stephens, was more optimistic when he said, "*Calvert-Dale is not going out of the flower business altogether, just the growing end. We might start up new greenhouses in Huttonville or Norval. I personally don't feel the growing end is going to die in the Brampton area. Someone is going to have to provide the rose production when Calvert-Dale stops growing*".[3] However, no one did. During the salvage operation, an Alton nursery purchased one of the Dale greenhouses and moved it to its location in Caledon for the production of bedding plants for the Spring market. It is still in use today, but most of the remaining greenhouses in the vast Calvert-Dale Estate were left to deteriorate. The skeletons of the structures were left open to the sky with broken panes and weeds their only crop. The site was a constant depressing reminder to many Bramptonians of a floral past that had been destroyed by circumstances beyond their control.

The Calvert-Dale Estate was not the only florist business in town to run into difficulty during this time. In 1963 at the inauguration of the Brampton Flower Festival Parade, there had been 48 Brampton florists actively engaged in greenhouse production of flowers. In 1975 there were only 14.

> *Gerry Neudoerffer, who had been in the industry since 1929 on looking over his 10 greenhouses, said, "I wouldn't advise anyone to go into the flower growing business today. I'm barely making a profit. Nothing like it used to be. I have to work 70 hours a week just to make a living and I doubt if I could sell my business to anyone. Who would invest the money to keep it running?"4*

Most of the problems facing the Calvert-Dale Estate were also those that the smaller nurseries had to face, some of whom had been in business for over 40 years. Rising fuel costs with no corresponding price increases for their product meant that the former growers simply could not compete in the marketplace of the day. Consumers were not willing to pay the price for what it was costing the various nurseries to grow their flowers. An article printed in the local paper reported, *"Gregory's Greenhouses located on Frederick Street were sold and the 16,000 square feet of glass and the hothouses will be taken down for houses. The heating was too expensive. The cost of oil has almost doubled in the past year from $6,000 to $12,000 a year. Also, the prices of cut fresh flowers have failed to rise as fast as expenses have. For example, pompom chrysanthemums cost $1.50 a bunch in 1965 and today cost $2.00.* 5

More telling was the fact that modern methods of greenhouse operation had left behind the older generation of hothouse flower-growers. Peter Hughes, president of the Ontario Flower Growers Co-operative was quoted, *"Today in the new greenhouses, automatic sprinklers water the plants and flowers, automatic boilers sense when to turn on the steam, and automatic devices shade delicate plants at the right time. The result is a greenhouse, which is more efficient because it needs*

This current view looking west towards Main Street shows the houses that were built on the site of the former Dale greenhouses. This property, formerly known as "The Flats," is presently under development, 2007. Courtesy Dale O'Hara Collection

less manpower to run it. Cut flowers will have to increase in price or there won't be any locally grown flowers."[6] For most of the older nurseries, the old greenhouses with their loose fitting glass and old boilers simply could not compete with the modern greenhouses and they had little capital to modernize. The solution for most of them was to shut down their operations and sell their land to developers.

No Longer A Flower Company

For the multitude of large and small growers who had made Brampton "The Flower Town of Canada," the land on which their greenhouses were built was selling at between $100,000 and $200,000 per acre. It was obvious to everyone involved in the industry that any profit to be made was no longer in growing flowers.

In June 1976, the remaining 115 acres of land owned by Calvert-Dale were sold to Kingspoint Developments. In 1977, the florist supply business was sold, with the perishables going to William Corrigan Ltd. and the supplies to Waterdale Inc. These sales totalled over $7 million in revenue for the Calvert-Dale Estate, and in November 1979 the company office was moved to Hamilton. Although there was still a company called Calvert-Dale Ltd., the main income was from mortgage interest, rental income and the interest on loans. It now acted as a holding company with no resemblance to the operation that grew the multitude of roses, carnations, chrysanthemums and orchids or to the floral industry in which it had been famous.

A Town Landmark is Lost

In that same year, the Town of Brampton debated on whether to demolish or renovate the last vestige of the Dale Estate. The big Dale boiler house and chimney, long abandoned and ravaged by vandals, was all that was left of Brampton's premier flower-growing empire. The Town was faced with the decision to either tear the building down to make way for a westward extension of Vodden Street or to allow a private developer, Chelsea Homes Ltd., to renovate the boiler house as a mini mall with restaurants,

Remnant of Flowertown's past stands lonely awaiting verdict — renovation or destruction

Headline from the local paper in 1977 tells of the debate surrounding the last of the Dale landmarks. Courtesy RPA

office space and boutiques. At the time, there was little interest in retaining part of the town's heritage and to most, the boiler room and chimney were an eyesore, a danger to the public and an impediment to progress. The Town Council decided to demolish the famous landmark. The following year, the bricks came tumbling down although it took many attempts to completely demolish the chimney such was the strength of its construction. All tangible evidence of the former Dale Estate ceased to exist and new roads were constructed, old roads were renamed and a 50-year-old landmark disappeared.[7]

The once mighty boiler room and chimney were abandoned and vandalized, leading to their eventual destruction in 1977.
Courtesy RPA

The Company Collapses

By 1980 the Calvert-Dale Estate audit showed assets of only $100,000 and shortly thereafter, the company was collapsed. The shares were practically valueless and anyone who had invested in the company was left with almost meaningless pieces of paper. Over the previous 20 years the company had continuously changed directors and officers and brought in new investors and major shareholders. Many of the top management profited greatly from the sale of the land and assets of the Dale Estate and W.E. Calvert Ltd and for them it was a good investment with a good return. For others directly involved in the company, it left a bitter taste and unanswered questions. Unfortunately, it was the complete demise of the Dale Estate and the end of the floral industry that had been so much a part of the fabric of Brampton.

Notes

1 Calvert Collection; RPA
2 Calvert Collection; RPA
3 *The Times and Conservator*; RPA
4 *The Times and Conservator*; RPA
5 *The Daily Times*; RPA
6 *The Daily Times*; RPA
7 *The Guardian*; Etheldale Sivell Collection

Chapter 12

The Legacy of the Dale Estate
The Present

When you walk through the neighbourhood of Main and Vodden streets in the northern part of the city of Brampton, you will not see any tangible evidence of the once great empire of the Dale Estate. The "acres of glass" that were symbolic of the town have been replaced with housing developments. Where once Harry Dale's house stood, surrounded by his beloved greenhouses, there is now a strip mall, ironically housing a florist shop that regularly advertises imported Columbian roses for $13.99 a dozen.

The northeast corner of Main and Vodden, once home to the Dales, is now a strip mall, 2007.
Courtesy Dale O'Hara Collection

A Great Canadian Story

The Dale Estate was a great Canadian company, started with an entrepreneurial spirit and nurtured with hard work and dedication, which allowed it to grow to be the best in the floral business. The Dales were ahead of their time in that they knew that the way to keep good employees and to maintain a successful enterprise was to treat people fairly and with respect. Their existence influenced the

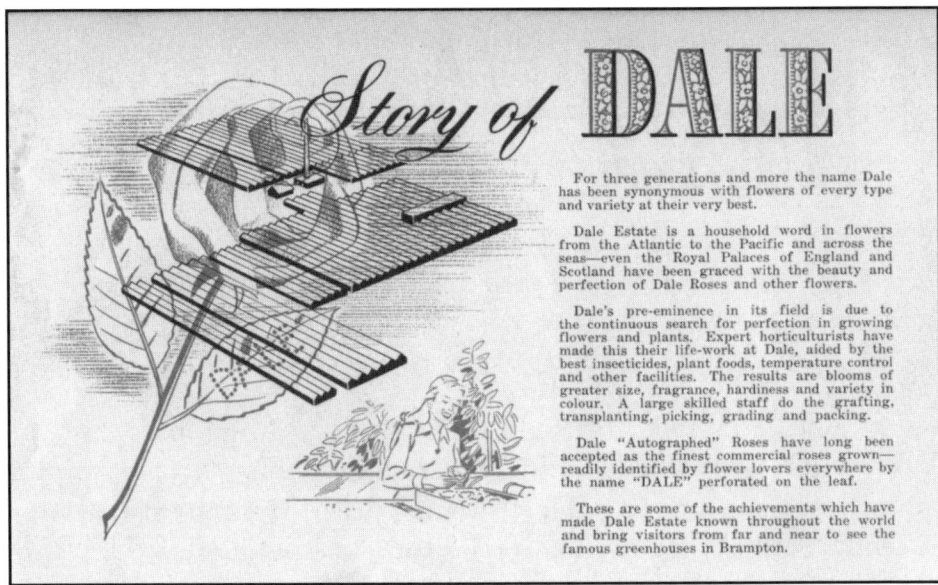

For three generations and more the name Dale has been synonymous with flowers of every type and variety at their very best.

Dale Estate is a household word in flowers from the Atlantic to the Pacific and across the seas—even the Royal Palaces of England and Scotland have been graced with the beauty and perfection of Dale Roses and other flowers.

Dale's pre-eminence in its field is due to the continuous search for perfection in growing flowers and plants. Expert horticulturists have made this their life-work at Dale, aided by the best insecticides, plant foods, temperature control and other facilities. The results are blooms of greater size, fragrance, hardiness and variety in colour. A large skilled staff do the grafting, transplanting, picking, grading and packing.

Dale "Autographed" Roses have long been accepted as the finest commercial roses grown— readily identified by flower lovers everywhere by the name "DALE" perforated on the leaf.

These are some of the achievements which have made Dale Estate known throughout the world and bring visitors from far and near to see the famous greenhouses in Brampton.

Courtesy RPA

development of a small Ontario town and, because of their presence, many other smaller companies in the same industry were able to grow and profit. It is evidence of the depth and solidity of the company that, despite personal tragedies within the Dale family, two World Wars, a flu pandemic and the greatest economic depression the world had seen, the Dale Estate continued to prosper for over 100 years.

Changing Times

Flowers were a product that was considered a necessity to the consumers of the era of the Dale Estate, but with modern times, they became a "luxury" item purchased only on special occasions. The world of Harry Dale and T.W. Duggan changed and Brampton changed with it. In an interview with Harry's granddaughter, Elizabeth Brydon Dickson, she summed up the situation with a comparison, *"When I was a youngster there were several companies making horse whips. You don't see any of those around anymore do you?"* An industry begun in a time of cheap labour and cheap fuel was overcome by demographic changes that swept the world in the mid-fifties. From a population of approximately 8,000 in 1949, Brampton has grown to over 400,000 in a span of 58 years. Rising oil prices, population explosions, different consumer tastes, transportation costs, rising real estate prices and corporate acquisitions and takeovers undermined any chance of the survival of the florist industry, and the Dale Estate in particular, in Brampton. Given these changes it was inevitable that flowers could no longer be grown on the scale that they had been for the previous 100 years.

A Forgotten Industry

Today large successful family-run enterprises are continually being taken over by bigger companies. Few manage to survive intact and their identity is usually lost. The pattern is repeated in company after company. Success attracts the bigger firm's acquisition team, the smaller company is purchased, the management is "re-assigned" and eventually let go. At some point the assets of the smaller enterprise are re-sold, and a profit is made for the parent company. Smaller is often better if a company wants to survive, but only if the economics of the time permit. In an interview with a local newspaper, Gord Fendley of Fendley's Florist said, *"Our smaller firm which has been at the same location since 1919, survived because we never got that big that anybody would want to buy us out. The big firms just couldn't afford to keep their greenhouses and were forced to sell."*[1] Fendley's also have since shut down their greenhouses and is strictly a retail florist shop selling imported flowers and plants. Such is our world of progress.

The northwest intersection of Main and Vodden streets where once stood the mighty Dale boiler house and chimney, 2007.
Courtesy Dale O'Hara Collection

Harry Dale's once great floral empire rose and fell with the times and nothing is left to remind people of the sea of glass which stretched over 40 acres of Brampton — not a street name, not a greenhouse, not a building or a commemorative plaque. Of the smaller nurseries and florists that proliferated in the shadow of the

Dale Estate, none remain. Few people are left who remember why Brampton earned its well-deserved reputation as "The Flower Town of Canada." It was as if the entire industry had never existed.

The Flower City Strategy

The City of Brampton's current logo; a stylized rose.
Courtesy City of Brampton

However, the millennium swept in a new outlook and attitude in Brampton's City Council. For many years Brampton's core area had been deteriorating with little to differentiate it as a city of note within the Greater Toronto Area. The absence of the greenhouses and the floral industry left the City floundering for an identity. In 2002 the City Council, under the direction and vision of Mayor Susan Fennell, received and approved The Flower City Strategy, *"with the expressed purpose of recapturing Brampton's floral heritage and once again being known as the Flower City of Canada; a city where all citizens recognize and celebrate their floral heritage and Brampton is known as the national tourist destination of choice."*[2]

The newly constructed Rose Theatre opened its doors to the public in September 2006. Courtesy City of Brampton

Modern-day Brampton is noted for its beautiful parks and floral displays.
Courtesy City of Brampton

The City has attempted to accomplish this by the rose symbol with which it chooses to identify itself. Harry's rose, famous as a symbol of quality and industriousness is an apt logo for the vibrant city. By naming the new theatre for the performing arts, the Rose Theatre, the City has continued its branding and has constructed a magnificent building of beauty and artistic merit. In 2006 Brampton successfully won Canada's Community in Bloom competition with special mention being made of the city's stunning floral displays. This annual affair harkens back to the days when the Dale Estate repeatedly won international awards for excellence and innovation. The multitude of magnificent flower displays that yearly grace its streets, parks and boulevards are helping to regain the city's floral reputation, and Brampton is well on its way to recapturing its past fame and can begin to again call itself "The Flower City of Canada."

A Heritage Worth Remembering

Many descendants of former employees and of the Dale family still choose to live in Brampton, with memories of a small town, green-houses and flowers that were a part of their everyday lives. Some of the wonderful original homes owned by the Dale ancestors can still be seen in the older area of Brampton. Harry did not grow his roses for the love of profit, but rather for his unabashed love of the rose itself. When the Dale greenhouses were shut down, most of the rose bushes were simply thrown out or left to die. Several of the employees and other townspeople retrieved some of the bushes and carefully nurtured them in their backyards where to this day they still grow and continue their prolific blooming year after year. The rootstock was hardy and hence Harry's roses have survived.

Few endeavors in life stand the test of time as permanent monuments to mankind's achievements and Dales was no exception. However, the company has left as its legacy a heritage worth remembering. Its business practices of fairness and respect, of prompt service and dedication are still qualities worthy of aspiration. Its legacy of beauty is reflected in the city's floral infrastructures of parks, valley corridors, streetscapes and gateways. The "acres of glass" and the roses which became the symbol of quality and beauty are remembered with pride. A small Ontario town, "The Flower Town of Canada," made famous by Harry Dale and the Dale Estate, is remembered and celebrated as an important part of Brampton's heritage.

Notes

---

1. *The Daily Times;* RPA
2. City of Brampton Publication

Epilogue

"If we do not know where we came from and reflect upon our past, it is difficult to go forward into our rapidly changing future."

A few years ago when I started writing this book, I received a phone call from someone who had retrieved a Dale rose bush in the 1970s when the company abandoned its greenhouses. She was a long-time resident of Brampton, knew of my connection to the family, and graciously gave me the bush, as she was moving to the West Coast. After quite a hilarious experience of digging up and planting the rose bush, it is now happily growing in my rose garden. Each year it gets stronger, producing beautiful deep red roses.

Harry Dale was my great-grandfather and I share with him not only his birth date, but also his abiding love and fascination with roses. Of all the multitude of flowers that he grew, roses were the ones that captured his heart, as any rosarian will understand. Their scent, their form, their colour never fail to enchant and lift my spirits and I hope that many other of Harry's roses, which are growing in Brampton backyard gardens, are bringing the same joy to their owners.

While I was growing up in Brampton, our family received a box of fresh flowers from the Dale Estate each week and my mother always let me arrange them. Bouquets of roses, carnations, daffodils, tulips and mums graced every corner of our home, filling my childhood years with their delicate perfume. My memories of playing in the greenhouses, the shipping room scented with

Harry Dale, Florist; born January 13, 1851; died July 15, 1900. Courtesy RPA

fresh flowers, my father's busy office, the scary tunnels under the main street, the hissing of the steam which heated my grandmother's house and those endless rows of glass stretching all over the north end of the town are integral to who I am.

Acres of Glass:
The Dale Estate covered
40 acres in greenhouses,
the largest of its kind on
the North American
continent, c.1960.
Courtesy RPA/Photograph Tom
Brydon

While nothing concrete remains of the once great Dale Estate, it is apparent that this company, the people who worked there and those who lived in its shadow, have had a great influence on the development of what is now the City of Brampton. As Tommy Thomson requested, *Acres of Glass* is my attempt to ensure that the history of the Dales and that of Brampton are not forgotten. I am pleased that I have been able to share these memories.

Dale Dickson O'Hara

Appendix I

A Long-Lost Dale Rose
From Harry With Love

The phone rang just as I was rushing out the door to the Inglewood Garden Club meeting. "Is this Dale O'Hara?" the voice said. "This is Barb Moore. We went to high school together."

I frantically searched my memory but came up absolutely blank. I had gone to Brampton High School back in the 1950s but this was 2004! Names and faces from that distant past often eluded me.

"I saw the recent article in the *Brampton Guardian* that said you were writing a book about the Dale Estate and were asking people to come forward with any stories or memorabilia that they might have. Well, I have an original Dale rose bush growing in my garden."

I couldn't quite believe what I was hearing. The Dale Estate, my family's business, after a century of growing roses for the North American market, had completely disappeared. Nothing remained. Not a greenhouse, not a building and certainly not the rose stock.

"That's amazing!" I replied. "Would you mind if I came and took a picture of it?"

"Well, that's what I'm calling about," she said. "I'm moving to the West Coast to be near my sister and I'd like you to have it."

A stunned silence hung on the line. I couldn't believe it! To have an actual rose bush, a tangible piece of my heritage, in my own garden, was too much to contemplate. I was beside myself with joy!

"That would be simply marvellous. Could I come and get it this afternoon?"

I didn't want her to change her mind and I was extremely anxious to actually see a real live Dale rose! And so we made a date for later that day.

You can imagine my excitement as I drove that morning to the Garden Club monthly meeting. They, of course, knew that I had a passion for roses and that I was writing a book about the Dale

Estate, which, during the first half of the 20th century, was the largest cut flower greenhouse operation in the world. The gist of the story was that my great-great grandfather, Edward Dale, had immigrated to Canada in 1863 with his young family and started a humble market garden business in Brampton, Ontario. His son Harry, my great-grandfather, from an early age had a fascination and love for roses. He began growing them in a tiny dugout greenhouse, peddling them door to door in the village along with the family's vegetable produce and from this small beginning, the flower business grew to 35 acres under glass. Annually, over five million roses were shipped worldwide and the company was renowned for their high quality long-stemmed red roses, autographed with the family name DALE.

I had grown up playing in the greenhouses where three generations of my extended family had all been involved in the business of the Dale Estate. Within a span of 10 years, starting in 1963, everything totally disappeared. Not a greenhouse was left and certainly no roses survived. It was an amazing story that had never been written and, as the keeper of the family records, the one who had an abiding love of roses and bore the name Dale, I had decided to write it all down. And here I was, in June of 2004, about to have in my possession an original Dale rose bush!

As I told my garden club friends of my excitement, I asked for their advice on how I should move the plant, as early summer was not the best time of year to transplant roses.

The spiritual environmentalist in the group solemnly advised that I should quietly walk up to the rose bush, introduce myself, and gently ask its permission to be moved.

What if it says no, I thought. "To heck with that!" I said. "I'm moving it regardless of what it wants!"

"You're not planning to move this on your own are you?" another lady asked.

"Well yes," I replied.

"I don't know how you're going to do it because a rose that old will have huge roots and you're going to have to dig down at least four to six feet and about a six foot radius. I don't know how you're going to be able to move all of that by yourself!" she exclaimed. Now I was getting quite worried. I had visions of a rather small three-foot hybrid tea and I was now being faced with the spectre of a backhoe being required.

"Extra feed," one said.

"Only move it at night," advised another.

"Don't let the roots touch the air!" exclaimed a third.

"Take a huge bucket," said the last.

So armed and ready, later that afternoon I made my way to Brampton. I wore my oldest clothes and brought every gardening tool I could think of. I stopped in at a local store and bought bags of the very best rose soil and the biggest basket I could find. With barely controlled excitement I approached the street address I had been given and knocked on the door. It opened to a woman whom I vaguely remembered from my past. Time had intervened and we both were older and heavier than our former teenage selves.

"Come in," she said, "and have a cup of coffee."

I didn't really want to. I just wanted to get on with seeing that rose for the first time, digging it up and taking it home. However, good manners won out and I sat for the next half hour and listened to Barb talk about people I didn't know, times I couldn't remember, and a past we shared but at different stages in our lives. I finally managed to turn the conversation to the reason I was there, namely the Dale rose.

She had come upon the rose bush in the mid to late sixties. When the greenhouses of the Dale Estate were destroyed and abandoned, all of the rose bushes were ripped out and dumped in a huge pile. She and her girlfriend, Donnadale Fendley, who coincidently is a thrice-removed cousin of mine, rescued a couple of the bushes and Barb came home and planted hers in her mother's garden. The bush had been there ever since, blooming repeatedly year after year. I mentally did the math and figured that it was approximately 50 years old at this time. Visions of a ten-foot root system filled my head. Whatever was I going to do?

"Well Barb, I'd better get going and get this rose bush dug up," I said.

I didn't want to appear too greedy but I wanted to get my hands on that Dale rose and I realized I had my work cut out for me!

"Oh," she said. "I've already dug it up for you. It's just outside."

"Curious," I thought. "How could she ever have managed such a large bush? She's a bit overweight and has just told me that her knees are full of arthritis and she can't manage either stairs or her gardens any more."

We went out to the front and I looked around. I saw nothing that even resembled a rose bush.

"Where is it?" I asked.

"There," she pointed.

Lying on its side beside her parked car, in the bright June sun, was a small, one-foot high rose bush, whose root system equalled it in length. The leaves were drooping and wilted as it lay on the hot asphalt of the driveway. The bare roots, bereft of any soil, lay open to the burning sun.

What could I say? I wanted to cry. All of my plans of gently removing it from its garden nest, asking its permission, digging deeply into the soil, being careful not to expose the roots were gone. I mumbled my thanks, said my goodbyes, hastily put the bush in the trunk of my car and drove off.

I managed to drive slowly until I was about two streets away and then I quickly pulled over to the side of the road. I jumped out of the car and raced around to the trunk. I lifted the lid and gently picked up the bush cradling it in my arms like a small child.

"I'm sorry, so sorry! It wasn't my fault. Really! I am SO SORRY!"

I kept repeating this phrase out loud as a mantra as I placed the bush, oh so carefully, into the basket of soil in the trunk. I was hoping it heard me and forgave the harsh treatment it had received. I promised it I would take care of it from here on in. It really was a pathetic little specimen. My vision of a magnificent rose bush growing straight and tall, blooming profusely was totally shattered.

When I arrived home, I had planned to put the bush at my back door but I changed my mind and decided to put it in my bigger garden with my more mature roses, hoping that it would garner strength from their presence. I found myself, like my spiritual friend, talking to this tiny bush the entire time, telling it how happy I was to have found it and to please, please, please, grow.

Never has a rose bush been planted so lovingly.

Never has a rose bush had such care.

I thought I'd given it the best possible chance to survive the transplanting.

I was wrong.

That night, a freak change in the weather plummeted the temperature from a high of 80F to a low of 40F with a predicted chance of frost in outlying areas.

"Oh no," I thought. "After everything that rose bush has gone through today, it will surely never survive this!"

So, there I was, in the clear moonlight of a summer's night, in my pyjamas and housecoat, feet in Wellington boots and carrying a large blue blanket. I tenderly tucked the edges of the blanket around and totally covered my tiny little rose bush. Fortunately only the heavens above could see my mad midnight behaviour.

"Good luck!" I whispered. "You're on your own."

The next morning, I rushed out to see how my Dale rose had fared. I hoped for the best. I expected the worst. I carefully pulled back the blue blanket that was covered in frost. And there it was.

Its sturdy little stem and four leaves were upright and perkily reaching for the summer sun.

"Welcome to my garden and welcome back to our family," I whispered.

Since then, the Dale rose has survived three winters. That first summer it had one bloom and the second it had three. The third year it produced stronger stems and this year it has once again survived a harsh winter. The bloom is a wonderful true red and a local rose specialist by the name of Jim Anderson has told me that it is probably the American Beauty that was the Dale Estate's most hardy specimen. It was this rose variety that gave them their international reputation.

I look forward to the day that perhaps I can actually take cuttings from the bush, stamp it with the DALE logo and proudly display my own long-stemmed rose.

My great-grandfather, Harry Dale, would have been proud.

The long-lost Dale Rose, June 2006. Courtesy Dale O'Hara

From an article by Dale O'Hara that originally appeared in *Family History Magazine* (January 2006 No. 126)

Appendix II

THE DALE ANCESTORS
OF DALE DICKSON O'HARA

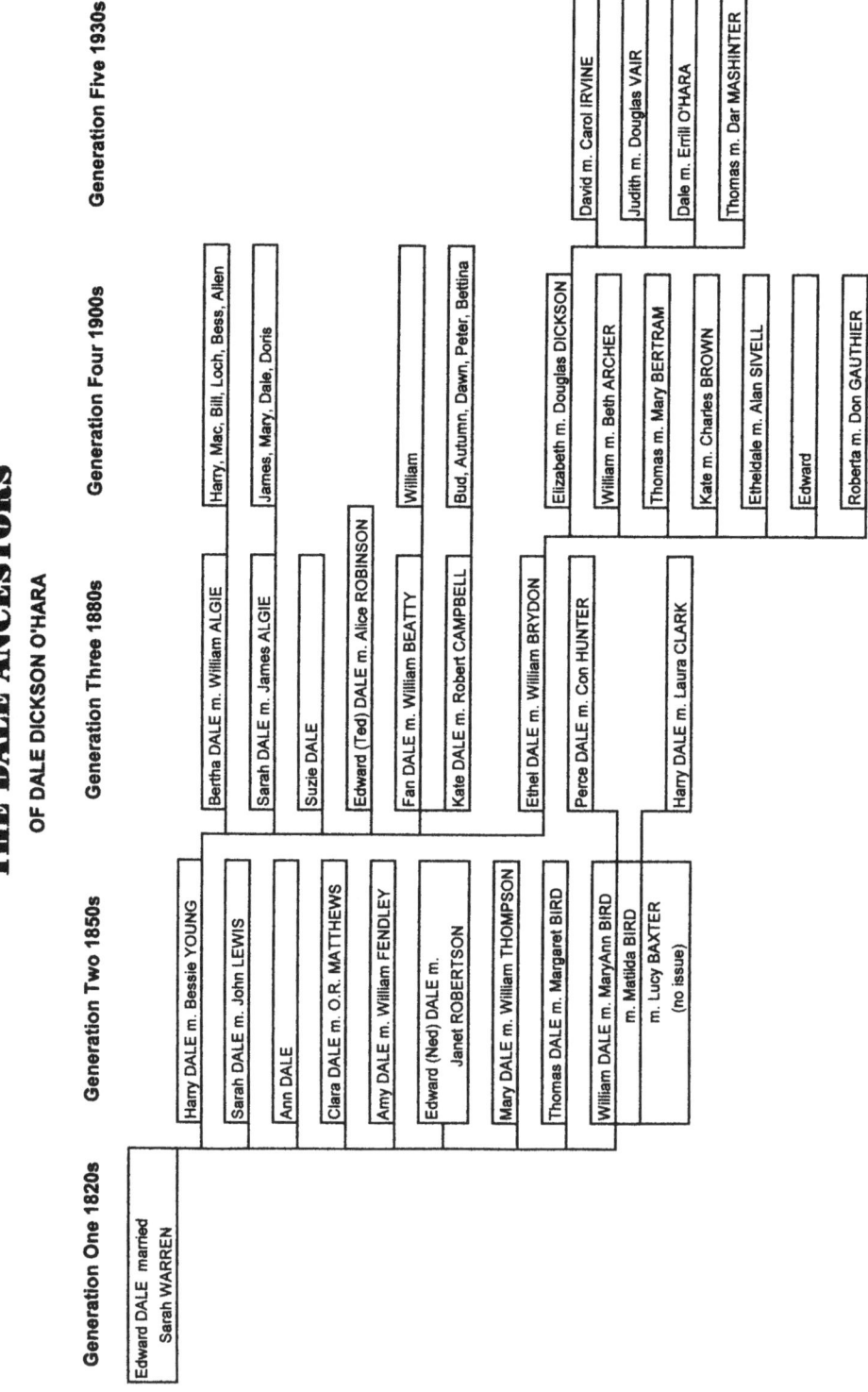

Generation One 1820s	Generation Two 1850s	Generation Three 1880s	Generation Four 1900s	Generation Five 1930s
Edward DALE married Sarah WARREN	Harry DALE m. Bessie YOUNG	Bertha DALE m. William ALGIE	Harry, Mac, Bill, Loch, Bess, Allen	
	Sarah DALE m. John LEWIS	Sarah DALE m. James ALGIE	James, Mary, Dale, Doris	
	Ann DALE	Suzie DALE		
	Clara DALE m. O.R. MATTHEWS	Edward (Ted) DALE m. Alice ROBINSON		
	Amy DALE m. William FENDLEY	Fan DALE m. William BEATTY	William	
	Edward (Ned) DALE m. Janet ROBERTSON	Kate DALE m. Robert CAMPBELL	Bud, Autumn, Dawn, Peter, Bettina	
	Mary DALE m. William THOMPSON	Ethel DALE m. William BRYDON	Elizabeth m. Douglas DICKSON	David m. Carol IRVINE
	Thomas DALE m. Margaret BIRD	Perce DALE m. Con HUNTER	William m. Beth ARCHER	Judith m. Douglas VAIR
	William DALE m. MaryAnn BIRD m. Matilda BIRD m. Lucy BAXTER (no issue)	Harry DALE m. Laura CLARK	Thomas m. Mary BERTRAM	Dale m. Errill O'HARA
			Kate m. Charles BROWN	Thomas m. Dar MASHINTER
			Etheldale m. Alan SIVELL	
			Edward	
			Roberta m. Don GAUTHIER	

158   The Dale Ancestors

Appendix III

THE DALE ESTATE STATISTICS 1863-1980				
YEAR	POPULATION	GREENHOUSES	PRODUCTION	OTHER
1863	1,200 est.		Market gardening	
1870		1 dugout type 12 x 40	First rose produced	
1874	2,718			Creation of *Edward Dale and Son*
1880-85	2,973	2 greenhouses		Creation of *Harry Dale Florist*
1891-93	3,000 est.	17,000 sq. ft. of glass	500,000 cut roses	Prize awarded
1895		7 greenhouses		T.W. Duggan hired
1896	3,070	65,000 sq. ft. of glass 8 greenhouses		
1897		90,000 sq. ft. 11 greenhouses		30 employees
1898		125,000 sq. ft. of glass 12 greenhouses	Mainly roses, carnations and chrysanthemums	
1899		150,000 sq. ft. of glass 20 greenhouses		
1900	3,100 est.	190,000 sq. ft. of glass		40 employees
1903		250,000 sq. ft. of glass 21 greenhouses		
1905	3,150 est.	450,000 sq. ft. of glass		150 employees
1908			10 million blooms annually	
1910	3,201	850,000 sq. ft. of glass		7,500 tons of coal at $120k per year
1911		20 acres under glass; first orchid house constructed	Roses, carnations, orchids, valley, lilies, mums, etc.	First orchids grown
1913	3,333 est.	1.25 million sq. ft. of glass total of 10 orchid houses	35,000 orchid plants	205 employees 9,000 tons of coal
1915		26 acres under glass	60,000 orchid plants	Own 127 acres of land
1919	3,600	1.4 million sq. ft. of glass 27 acres under glass	12.5 million blooms yearly	100 acres involved in floriculture 220 employees 12,000 tons of coal 3rd largest greenhouses in the world

THE DALE ESTATE STATISTICS 1863-1980 continued				
Year	Population	Greenhouses	Production	Other
1921-25	4,551		1 million cultivated plants 30 varieties of flowers 20 different kinds of roses	Dales incorporated Own 140 acres farmland 350 employees 16,000 tons coal annually
1927		35 acres under glass 8 miles of greenhouses		27 miles of walkways Total of 243 acres owned 19,000 tons coal annually
1933				T.W. Duggan retires
1934	5,700			Autographed Rose introduced
1935			4.5 million roses 1.5million carnations 1 million lily of valley 1.5 million bulbs 700,000 chrysanthemums 250,000 orchids 200,000 lilies	100,000 hot house tomatoes 10,000 English cucumbers 500 different varieties of orchids 225 acre farmland/55 cattle
1938		9 miles greenhouses 35 acres under glass 132 greenhouses	10 million blooms 5 million roses 4 acres of asparagus for greenery	400 employees 1 mile of tunnels 32 miles of walkways 100 miles steam pipes
1940-43	6,020			20 tons of ice annually Chimney height 300'
1947	6,750	1.5 million sq. ft. of glass	1.5 million carnations 200,000 orchids	100,000 lb. tomatoes 10,000 cucumbers 250 acres of farmland
1948	6,783		120,000 rose grafts yearly	20,000 tons of coal 125 cattle for fertilizer
1949	8,000	140 greenhouses	5.75 million cut roses 40,000 graded daily	Converted to oil, 15,000 gal. daily 25% of town linked to Dales
1953	10,366	132 greenhouses Each orchid house is 200 feet long	13 million blooms 7 million cut roses (50,000 cut daily) 200,000 orchid plants 1/3 acre of orchids	350 employees 2.5 miles of pipe for fertilizer
1955	11,758	8 additional greenhouses		

THE DALE ESTATE STATISTICS 1863-1980 continued				
YEAR	**POPULATION**	**GREENHOUSES**	**PRODUCTION**	**OTHER**
1956	13,009	140 greenhouses 40 acres of greenhouses and buildings 1.5 million sq. ft. of glass	20 million blooms total 10 million cut roses 10 million mums, orchids, carnations, tulips, daffodils, lilies, snapdragons, gardenias, stephanotis, stocks, potted plants, azaleas, hydrangeas, poinsettias, rose bushes, palms and ferns	350 employees
1957-58	14,374			Dales Flowerland opens
1961	24,363	140 greenhouses 35 acres under glass	20 million blooms 9 million cut roses 32 varieties of flowers and plants 100,000 orchids; 17,500 orchid plants	Dale Estate sold Own 340 acres of land 360 employees Wholesale warehouses in Toronto and Montreal
1963	26,363			48 independent growers in Brampton area
1965	36,000	Combined Calvert-Dale is 40 acres under glass/1.8 million sq. ft. of glass		Combined with W.E. Calvert Ltd. 573 employees combined
1968	37,701	300,000 sq. ft. closed		
1972		6.7 acres released for development		
1974-76	46,386	Major greenhouses phased out Land sold for housing	Most rose and flower production stopped	315 employees terminated Oil cost $1 million per year
1976-77		Remaining assets sold (115 acres land and florist supply)		
1979		Holding company office moved to Hamilton		Destruction of Dale chimney
1980		Ceased to exist on TSE		
Most of these statistics were gleaned from company reports. They are to be viewed as estimates only.				

Appendix IV

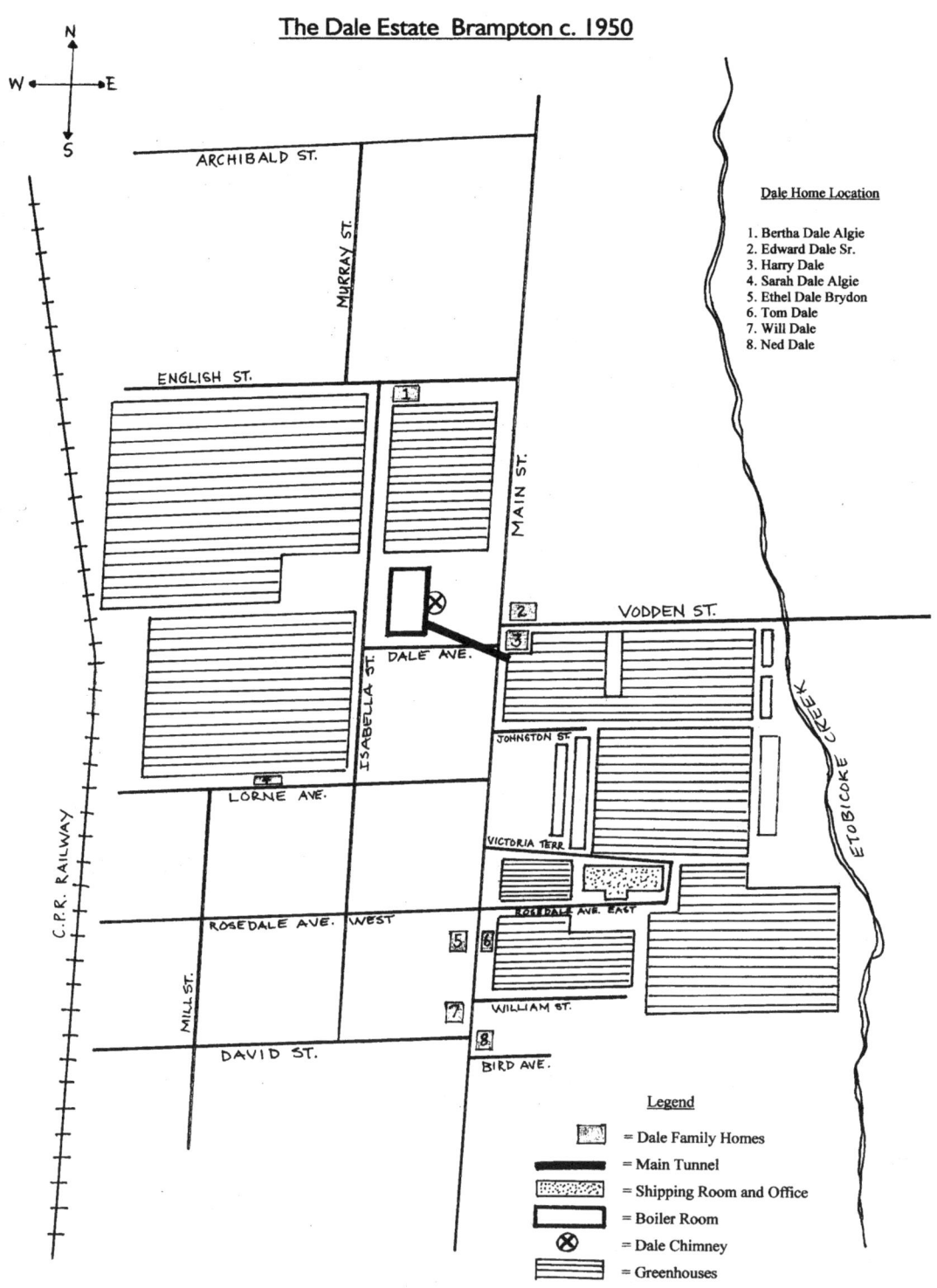

The Dale Estate Brampton c. 1950

Dale Home Location

1. Bertha Dale Algie
2. Edward Dale Sr.
3. Harry Dale
4. Sarah Dale Algie
5. Ethel Dale Brydon
6. Tom Dale
7. Will Dale
8. Ned Dale

ARCHIBALD ST.

MURRAY ST.

ENGLISH ST.

MAIN ST.

VODDEN ST.

ISABELLA ST.

DALE AVE.

JOHNSTON ST.

VICTORIA TERR.

LORNE AVE.

C.P.R. RAILWAY

ROSEDALE AVE. WEST

ROSEDALE AVE. EAST

MILL ST.

WILLIAM ST.

DAVID ST.

BIRD AVE.

ETOBICOKE CREEK

Legend

= Dale Family Homes

= Main Tunnel

= Shipping Room and Office

= Boiler Room

⊗ = Dale Chimney

= Greenhouses

The City of Brampton 2007

Courtesy City of Brampton Planning Department

Bibliography

Cairns, Dr. Tommy. *Ortho's All About Roses*. Meredith Publishing Group, 1999

The Corporation of the County of Peel. *A History of Peel County 1867-1967*. Charters Publishing Company Ltd., 1967

The Corporation of the Town of Brampton and the Brampton Centennial Committee. *Brampton's 100th Anniversary 1873-1973*. Charters Publishing Company Ltd., 1973

Loverseed, Helga V., *Brampton: An Illustrated History*. Windsor Publications Ltd., 1987

Neff, M.S., *Effects of Storage Conditions on Cut Roses*. Botanical Gazette, Vol. 103, No. 4 (Jun., 1942), pp. 794-805. University of Chicago Press, 1942

Salisbury, Lionel and Rob. *Now and Then, a Photo Journey Through Brampton*. Self published, 1989

Archival Resources

Archives of Ontario, RG55-17-43-7 Copy Book (1-267): indexed, MS3594

Brampton Cemetery Records

Brampton Library Archives (Chinguacousy Branch) *Maclean's Magazine,* .S1924-1pf

Region of Peel Archives (hereafter RPA), Mary Beatty Collection, M1992

RPA, Wm. P. Bull Collection, M1991.045

RPA, Jack Calvert Collection, M1992

RPA, C. Chinn Collection

RPA, R. K. Cooper Collection, M1992.068

RPA, R. L. Frost Postcard Collection, M1991.028

RPA, Abstract Index for Chinguacousy Township, Registry Book CH90 1869-1920

RPA, Assessment Rolls 1877

RPA, Collector's Roll 1887-1907

RPA, Census 1860-1910

RPA, Copy Books 1861-1901

RPA, Estate Records Index #1924

RPA, Fire Insurance Plan 1924, 1934, 1940

RPA, Newspapers: *The Brampton Times, The Conservator, The Daily Times,* 90.000M, various issues from 1860-1980, microfilm

Toronto Public Library; T.R.L.; Special Collections, Baldwin Room, AR 690.89029 L59.2. Handbook of Commercial Greenhouses and Materials

Images have been used where appropriate to tell the story; for accurate dates of these images, contact the Region of Peel Archives.

Personal Collections

Personal Collection: Brenda Charters
Personal Collection: Ruth Edwards
Personal Collection: Glynne Everson
Personal Collection: Virginia Gould
Personal Collection: Dale O'Hara
Personal Collection: Etheldale Sivell
Personal Collection: Darren Spindler
Personal Collection: Jim Taylor

Personal Photo Collections

Personal Photo Collection: Thomas Brydon
Personal Photo Collection: Ben Cannons
Personal Photo Collection: Ruth Edwards
Personal Photo Collection: Douglas Fine
Personal Photo Collection: Philip Gauthier
Personal Photo Collection: Dale O'Hara
Personal Photo Collection: Etheldale Sivell
Personal Photo Collection: Darren Spindler
Personal Photo Collection: Jim Taylor
Personal Photo Collection: Marilyn Thomson
Personal Photo Collection: Iris Tuckey
Personal Photo Collection: Paul Willoughby

Personal Interviews

Fred Bacon, Ben Cannons, Brenda Duggan Charters, Elizabeth Brydon Dickson, Ruth Edwards, Glynne Everson, Harry Letton, Etheldale Brydon Sivell, Florence and Cliff Mowat, Bill Waters

Oral Histories

Virginia Algie, Don Beatty, Autumn Campbell, Bernice Colville, David Dickson, Dean Gowland, Alice Ann Train, Bonnie Fendley Martin, John Missud, Jean Stapleton, Iris Tuckey, Judith Vair

Web Resources

Genealogy search. http://www.ancestry.co.uk

Genealogy search. http://www.1837online.com

Genealogy search. http://www.freemd.org.uk

Genealogy search. http://www.familysearch.org

General Rose Information on Propagation, Manetti Rootstock, How to Care for Cut Roses. http://www.ars.org., http://www.gardenweb.com

"Key Economic Events in History of Canada." Government of Canada. http://www.canadianeconomy.gc.ca

"Key Economic Events 1914-1918-World War 1: Effect on the Canadian Economy." http://canadianeconoomy.gc.ca/english/economy/1914ww1.html

"Overview of Twentieth Century Canadian Economic Development." Trent University. http://www.trentu.ca

"The Crimean War: general causes." http//www.victorianweb.org

"The Great Boom of 1900 to 1913." Laurier House National Historic Site of Canada. http://www.pc.gc.ca

"The Great Depression of Canada." http://www.pc.gc.ca

"The Prairie Wheat Economy." University of Toronto. http://www.chass.toronto.edu

"The Orchid House." http://www.retirees.uwaterloo.ca

"The Story of the Great Influenza Pandemic of 1918." http://www.cnn.com/books/beginnings/9911/flu/

"Timeline of Ontario History." http://www.en.wikipedia.org

"Wages and Farming in Victorian England." Economy of Victorian England 1840-1860. http:// www.en.wikipedia.org

Index